Clothing
FASHION, FABRICS & CONSTRUCTION

Student Activity Manual

Mc Graw Hill **Glencoe**

New York, New York   Columbus, Ohio   Chicago, Illinois   Woodland Hills, California

Contributors

Holly Bohart
Freelance Writer/Editor
Ellicott City, Maryland

Susan C. Teelin
FCS Instructor
Camden, New York

Gayle McDowell
Freelance Writer
Peoria, Illinois

Christine Venzon
Freelance Writer
New Iberia, Louisiana

Art Credits

Art MacDillo's/Gary Skillestad and Renie Hanna

Safety Notice

The reader is expressly advised to consider and use all safety precautions described in the *Clothing: Fashion, Fabrics & Construction* program or that might also be indicated by undertaking the activities described herein. In addition, common sense should be exercised to help avoid all potential hazards and, in particular, to take relevant safety precautions concerning any known or likely hazards involved in using the procedures described in the *Clothing: Fashion, Fabrics & Construction* program.

Publisher and Authors assume no responsibility for the activities of the reader or for the subject matter experts who prepared this book. Publisher and Authors make no representation or warranties of any kind, including but not limited to, the warranties of fitness for particular purpose or merchantability, nor for any implied warranties related thereto, or otherwise. Publisher and Authors will not be liable for damages of any type, including any consequential, special or exemplary damages resulting, in whole or in part, from reader's use or reliance upon the information, instructions, warnings, or other matter contained in the *Clothing: Fashion, Fabrics & Construction* program.

Brand Name Disclaimer

Glencoe/McGraw-Hill does not necessarily recommend or endorse any particular company or brand name product that may be discussed in this manual. Brand name products are used because they are readily available, likely to be known to the reader, and their use may aid in the understanding of the book. Publisher recognizes other brand name or generic products may be substituted and work as well or better than those featured in the manual.

Contents

Chapter ──────── Unit 1: Clothing and Society ──────── Page

1 *Study Guide:* Influences on Clothing 7
Decision-Making Challenges 9

2 *Study Guide:* Cultures and Customs 11
Choices and Customs 13
Your Clothing Customs 14

3 *Study Guide:* Clothing and Families 15
Personal Budget 17

4 *Study Guide:* Clothing and Self-Expression 19
Your Clothing Personality 21
Analyzing Impressions 22

Unit 1 Activity: Is Fashion Promotion for You? 23

Unit 1 Activity: Fashion Promotion Career Paths 24

Chapter ──────── Unit 2: The Fashion World ──────── Page

5 *Study Guide:* Fashion History 25
Historical Influences on Fashion 27
Exploring Fashion History 28

6 *Study Guide:* Fashion Styles 29
Clothing Style Terms 31
Styles for Different Effects 32

7 *Study Guide:* Fashion Designers 33
Creating Fashion Designs 35

8 *Study Guide:* The Fashion Industry 37
The Manufacturing Process 39
Fashion Promotion Strategies 40

Unit 2 Activity: Is Apparel Production for You? 41

Unit 2 Activity: Constructing a Chronological Résumé 42

Chapter ──────── Unit 3: Color and Design ──────── Page

9 *Study Guide:* Understanding Color 43
Creating a Color Wheel 45
Color Schemes 47
Colors for You 48
Choosing Wardrobe Colors 49
Solving Color Problems 50

10 *Study Guide:* Understanding Design 51
Design Opinions 53
Analyzing Design 54
Fashion Design Solutions 55
Design and Your Image 56

Unit 3 Activity: Is a Career in Design for you? 57

Unit 3 Activity: Career Achievements—Looking Forward ... 58

Chapter ──────── Unit 4: Fibers and Fabrics ──────── Page

11 *Study Guide:* Textile Fibers 59
Fiber Characteristics 61
Studying Fibers 62

Contents

(continued)

Fiber Classifications 63

12   *Study Guide:* Fabric Construction 65

A Fabric Library 67

13   *Study Guide:* Fabric Finishes 69

Identifying Fabric Finishes 71

Fabric Finish Experiment 72

Unit 4 Activity: Is Textile Production for You? 73

Unit 4 Activity: Career Paths in Textile Production 74

Chapter	**Unit 5: Clothing Care**	Page

14   *Study Guide:* Clothing Care Basics 75

Stain Removal Experiment 77

15   *Study Guide:* Laundry and Dry Cleaning 79

Comparing Costs 81

Laundry Advice 82

16   *Study Guide:* Redesign, Repair, and Recycle 83

Fabric Dye Experiment 85

New Ideas for Clothes 86

Unit 5 Activity: Is Fashion Services for You? 87

Unit 5 Activity: Constructing a Skills-Based Résumé 88

Chapter	**Unit 6: Clothing Selection**	Page

17   *Study Guide:* Exploring Options 89

Taking a Wardrobe Inventory 91

Evaluating Needs and Wants 92

Expanding Your Wardrobe 93

18   *Study Guide:* Accessing Information 95

Advertising Appeals 97

Rating Your Shopping Skills 98

19   *Study Guide:* Evaluating Selections 99

Checking for Quality 101

Cost Per Wearing 102

20   *Study Guide:* Consumer Responsibilities 103

Writing a Complaint Letter 105

Consumer Protection Laws 106

21   *Study Guide:* Selecting Clothes for Others 107

Personal Shopper 109

Choosing Clothes for Others 111

Unit 6 Activity: Is Fashion Merchandising for You? 113

Unit 6 Activity: Writing a Letter of Inquiry 114

Chapter	**Unit 7: The Workplace**	Page

22   *Study Guide:* Career Preparation 115

Career Interviews 117

Job Application 119

Answering Interview Questions 121

23   *Study Guide:* Success on the Job 123

Qualities for Success 125

Contents

(continued)

	Retail Math Skills	126
24	*Study Guide:* Fashion Entrepreneurs	127
	Challenges and Opportunities	129
	Writing a Press Release	130
25	*Study Guide:* Global Marketplace	131
	Clothing Origins	133
	Unit 7 Activity: Is Communication and Education for You?	135
	Unit 7 Activity: Jobs in Communication and Education	136

Sewing and Serging Handbook

Lesson — **Part 1: Patterns, Fabrics, and Notions** — **Page**

1	*Study Guide:* Selecting a Pattern	137
	Choosing a Pattern	139
2	*Study Guide:* Selecting Fabric	141
	Comparing Fabrics	143
3	*Study Guide:* Selecting Notions	145
	Advice About Notions	147

Lesson — **Part 2: Machines and Equipment** — **Page**

4	*Study Guide:* Using a Sewing Machine	149
	Parts of a Sewing Machine	151
	Sewing Machine Knowledge	152
5	*Study Guide:* Using a Serger	153
	Parts of a Serger	155
	Serging Practice	156
6	*Study Guide:* Identifying Sewing Equipment	157
	Identifying Tools and Supplies	159
	Safety Rules	161

Lesson — **Part 3: Getting Ready to Sew** — **Page**

7	*Study Guide:* Understanding Patterns	163
	Using Patterns	165
	Identifying Pattern Markings	166
8	*Study Guide:* Adjusting a Pattern	167
	Pattern Adjustments	168
9	*Study Guide:* Preparing Fabric	169
	Fabric Preparation Checklist	170
10	*Study Guide:* Laying Out a Pattern	171
	Pattern Layout Procedure	172
11	*Study Guide:* Cutting and Marking Fabric	173
	Cutting and Marking Methods	174

Lesson — **Part 4: Basic Construction** — **Page**

12	*Study Guide:* Stitching by Machine	175
	Identifying Machine Stitches	176
13	*Study Guide:* Stitching by Hand	177
	Identifying Hand Stitches	178

Contents

(continued)

14 *Study Guide:* Pressing Fabric 179
   Pressing Pointers 180
15 *Study Guide:* Making Darts 181
   Quick Tips on Making Darts 182
16 *Study Guide:* Gathering and Easing Fabric 183
   Controlling Fullness 184
17 *Study Guide:* Sewing Plain Seams 185
   Practice with Plain Seams 186
18 *Study Guide:* Applying Facings 187
   Checkup on Facings 188
19 *Study Guide:* Making Casings 189
   Casing Practice 190
20 *Study Guide:* Applying Fasteners 191
   Buttonhole Math 192
   Fastener Practice 193
21 *Study Guide:* Putting in Zippers 195
   Zipper Application 196
22 *Study Guide:* Putting in Hems 197
   Hem Finishes 198
23 *Study Guide:* Checking the Fit 199
   Evaluating Quality and Fit 200

Lesson——————**Part 5: Special Sewing Techniques** ——————**Page**

24 *Study Guide:* Sewing Special Seams 201
   Identifying Special Seams 202
25 *Study Guide:* Making Tucks and Pleats 203
   Identifying Tucks and Pleats 204
26 *Study Guide:* Applying Interfacings 205
   Comparing Interfacings 206
27 *Study Guide:* Putting in Linings 207
   Questions About Linings 208
28 *Study Guide:* Sewing Collars 209
   Identifying Collars 210
29 *Study Guide:* Sewing Sleeves 211
   Identifying Sleeves 212
30 *Study Guide:* Sewing Cuffs 213
   Cuff Construction 214
31 *Study Guide:* Sewing Pockets 215
   Pocket Identification 216
32 *Study Guide:* Finishing Waistlines 217
   Waistband Checkup 218
33 *Study Guide:* Applying Bias Bindings 219
   About Bias Bindings 220
34 *Study Guide:* Adding Ruffles 221
   Making Ruffles 222
35 *Study Guide:* Adding Trims 223
   Comparing Trims 224

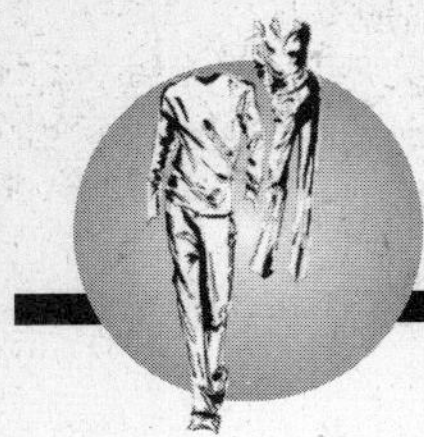

Choices and Customs

Directions: Read the following situations. Explain how customs and attitudes toward them are demonstrated in each one, using concepts discussed in the chapter.

1. A teen is dressing to go out with the family. He puts on a warm-up jersey like those worn by his favorite basketball team; fashionably baggy, knee-length jeans; and a new pair of popular athletic shoes. His parent tells him: "I thought you were going to wear something nice." The teen replies: "These are my best clothes."

____

____

____

2. A teen and her family are vacationing in a large coastal city. Before seeing a play downtown, they go to a very nice restaurant near the theater where the diners and wait staff alike are dressed formally. The next night, they eat at an equally fancy restaurant on the beach. There, sandals, sundresses, and flowered shirts are the clothing of choice.

____

____

____

3. A group of teens are shopping at the mall when they see their principal with her children buying a video. The teens are surprised by her dress: jeans, loafers, and a bright red sweatshirt with "World's Best Mom" stitched in plaid trim.

____

____

____

4. Walking across the high school campus, one teen stands out. Although the day is hot, she wears billowing pants, a straight, long-sleeved jacket, and a flowing headscarf. She knows that people think she is terribly uncomfortable. What really makes her uncomfortable, however, is the idea of wearing shorts and T-shirts.

____

____

____

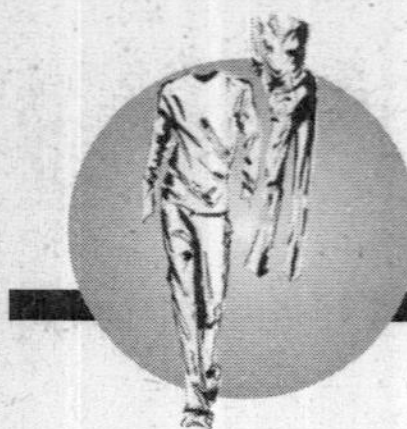

Your Clothing Customs

Directions: Describe typical outfits you would wear for the occasions in the chart below. In the last column explain why you make these choices. Then write your conclusions in the space provided below.

Occasion	Clothing	Reasons for Your Choices
Average school day		
After school		
Leisure time at home		
School dance		
Going out with friends		
Family member's wedding		
Dinner out with family		

Conclusions

Compare your responses in the chart to those of classmates. What similarities and differences do you notice? How do you account for them?

____

____

____

____

____

____

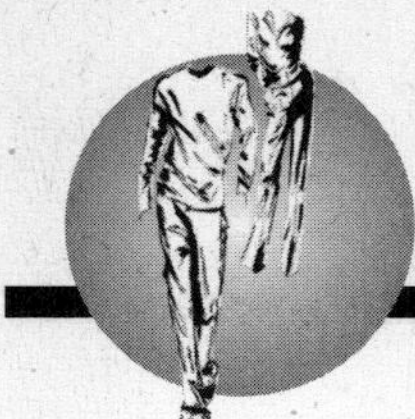

Clothing Style Terms

Directions: Match each description in the left column with the correct fashion term in the right column. Write the letter of the answer in the space provided. No term will be used more than once. Some terms will not be used.

Definitions

_____ 1. Dress with billowed effect created by gathering the bodice fullness and letting it fall over the waistline seam.

_____ 2. Close-fitting dress with no waistline seam and shaped by darts.

_____ 3. Hip-length jacket styled after those worn by sailors.

_____ 4. Soft, bias-cut neckline draped in the front or back.

_____ 5. Close-fitting, flared dress or coat that has no waistline; fit is achieved with seams.

_____ 6. Classic single- or double-breasted jacket.

_____ 7. Style of sleeve that is cut in one piece with the bodice.

_____ 8. Hip-length shirt style inspired by the ancient Romans.

_____ 9. Straight-cut, loose-fitting dress with no waistline seam.

_____ 10. Pants that look like a skirt.

_____ 11. Velvet-collared jacket named for a 19th-century earl.

_____ 12. Short, open jacket that ends above the waist.

_____ 13. Dress with a high waistline placed just below the bust.

_____ 14. One-piece garment that combines bodice and pants.

_____ 15. Shirt part that folds back to form a continuation of the collar.

_____ 16. Skirt formed by shaped panels.

_____ 17. Collarless jacket or sweater that buttons down the front.

_____ 18. Type of sleeve that is stitched into an armhole seam.

_____ 19. One-piece collar and lapel that form a continuous, curved line around the neck to the front closure of a garment.

_____ 20. Skirt or dress that falls to mid-thigh.

Terms

A. A-line
B. blazer
C. blouson
D. bolero
E. cardigan
F. chemise
G. chesterfield
H. cowl
I. culottes
J. empire
K. gored
L. henley
M. jumpsuit
N. kilt
O. kimono
P. lapel
Q. mini
R. pea
S. princess
T. raglan
U. set-in
V. shawl
W. sheath
X. shift
Y. sweetheart
Z. tunic

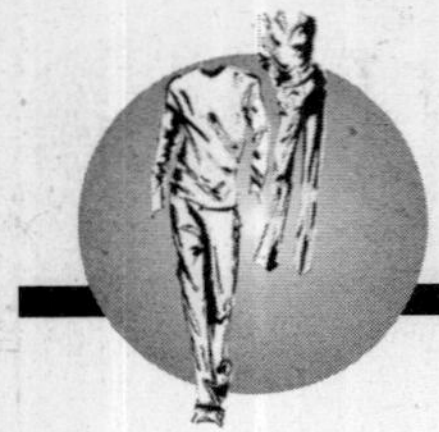

Styles for Different Effects

Directions: Using styles to achieve a certain look is one element of successful design. For each outfit below, suggest different garment styles and features that you would use to create the look indicated.

1. A romantic blouse and skirt: ____

____

____

____

____

2. Casual shirt and pants for men: ____

____

____

____

____

____

3. A professional suit for women: ____

____

____

____

____

____

4. An outfit that you would like to wear (describe the look and how you would achieve it): _______________

____

____

____

____

Clothing: Fashion, Fabrics & Construction Student Activity Manual
Copyright © by The McGraw-Hill Companies, Inc. All rights reserved.

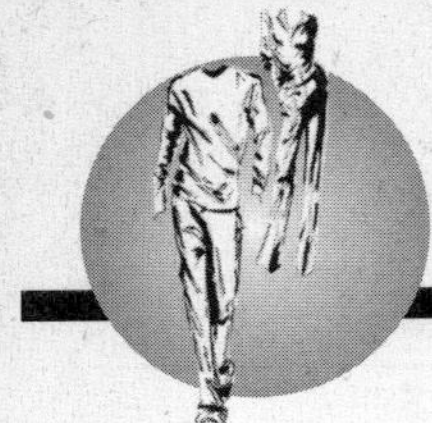

Fashion Designers

Directions: As you read the chapter, answer the following questions. Later you can use this study guide to review for the Chapter 7 test.

1. What areas of specialization exist in fashion design? _______________________________________

____

____

2. What is a fashion house? ____

3. Why might a designer produce several different collections for the same season? _______________

____

____

4. How do stylists cut costs when creating knock-offs? ______________________________________

____

____

5. What are the five steps in the design process? ____

____

____

____

6. What is the literal English translation of haute couture? What is its meaning in fashion? ________

____

____

____

7. How does a CAD system's three-dimensional dress form simplify trying out design changes? ______

____

____

____

(continued on next page)

Clothing: Fashion, Fabrics & Construction Student Activity Manual
Copyright © by The McGraw-Hill Companies, Inc. All rights reserved.

Chapter 7
Study Guide *(continued)*

8. How did World War II permanently change the fashion industry? ___________________________

____

____

9. Why do designers hold fashion shows? ____

____

____

10. What is a pret-a-porter collection? How many collections are presented per year? ___________

____

11. What is the relationship between a licensor and a licensee? _____________________________

____

____

12. Is the person whose name appears on a pair of "designer" sunglasses the same person who designed them? Explain.

____

____

13. In what type of clothing did Bill Blass specialize? ____________________________________

____

14. For what garments is "Coco" Chanel remembered? ____________________________________

____

15. Contrast the fashion designs of Betsey Johnson and Donna Karan. ______________________

____

____

16. From the list of "Famous Designers" on text pages 126 to 131, choose three of your favorite designers and identify why their designs appeal to you. If necessary, use an additional sheet of paper and attach it to this study guide.

____

____

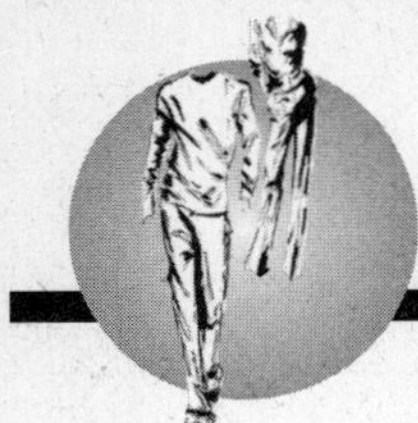

Creating Fashion Designs

Chapter 7
Activity

Directions: Sketching is the method designers use to communicate their fashion ideas. To try out your design creativity, think of an original garment design. Plan the outfit by answering the questions below. Then trace the figure on the next page and sketch your design on the tracing.

1. Who would the targeted customer be for your garment? ______________________________

   ____

2. What category will your design fit (casual; formal; high fashion; other)? ________________

   ____

3. Describe the garment you want to design. What styles from Chapter 6 will be included?________

   ____

   ____

   ____

   ____

4. What fabric(s) will be used in your design? Will they be solid colors or prints? Describe them. __________

   ____

   ____

   ____

5. Describe fasteners and trims that will be used on your garment. ________________________

   ____

   ____

   ____

6. Will your garment have any unique design details? Explain. ____________________________

   ____

   ____

   ____

(continued on next page)

Chapter 7
Activity (continued)

7. How will you accessorize your design? _______________________________

____

____

____

Sketching Your Design

Trace this figure onto other paper. You can
adapt the figure for a male or female garment
design. If you wish, you can also modify the
pose as you develop your design.

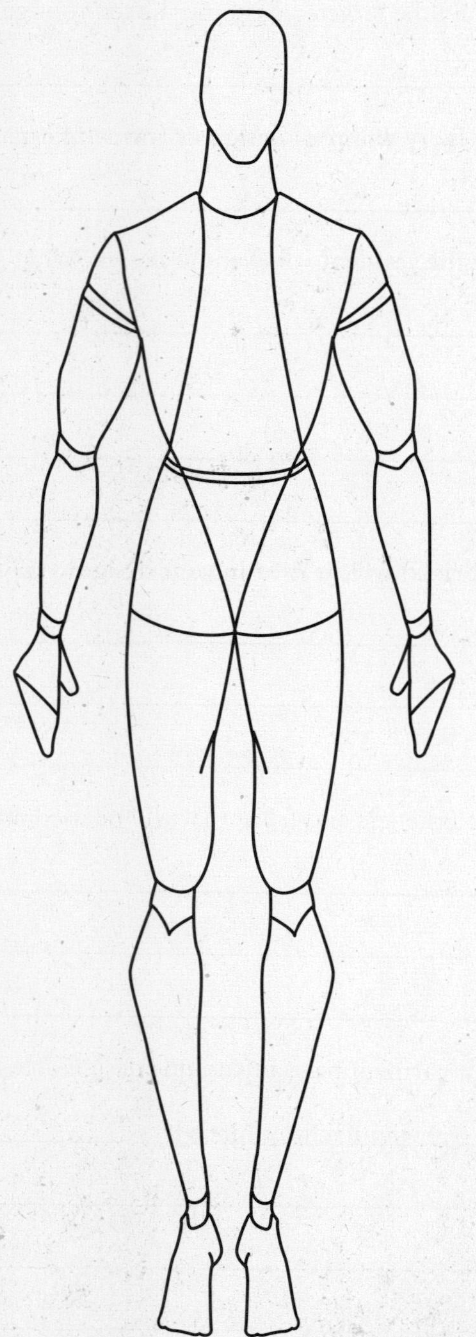

Clothing: Fashion, Fabrics & Construction Student Activity Manual

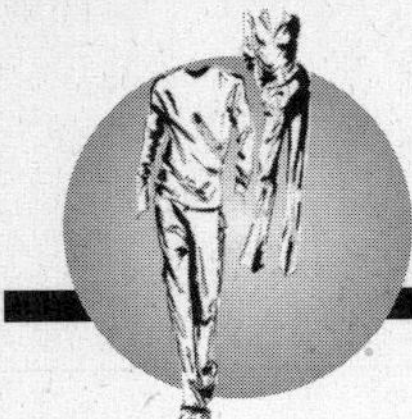

The Fashion Industry

Directions: As you read the chapter, answer the following questions. Later you can use this study guide to review for the Chapter 8 test.

1. List at least six uses for textiles other than for clothing. ___________________________________

____

____

2. Describe three different sources of textile fibers. ___________________________________

____

____

____

3. Why is research and development called "the backbone of the textile industry"? ___________________

____

____

4. What is the advantage of using a forecasting service? ___________________________________

____

____

5. How are textiles converted by a textile converter? ___________________________________

____

____

6. Why is the southeastern United States so important to the textile industry? ___________________

____

____

7. Why does a manufacturer hire a contractor? ___________________________________

____

____

(continued on next page)

Chapter 8
Study Guide (continued)

8. What costs are included to figure a garment's wholesale price? ___________________

____

____

9. What union represents garment workers in the United States? ___________________

____

____

10. What is the significance of Seventh Avenue in the garment industry? ___________

____

11. What is the role of fashion retailers? ______________________________________

____

12. What is direct retailing? Give two examples of direct retailing. _______________

____

____

13. Why does a store buyer check with the general merchandise manager before making a purchase? _________

____

____

14. How do marketers try to predict what consumers will need and want to buy? ___________

____

15. List resources that marketers use to promote their products and services. ___________

____

16. What role do fashion magazines play in the fashion industry? Name two fashion magazines ___________

____

____

____

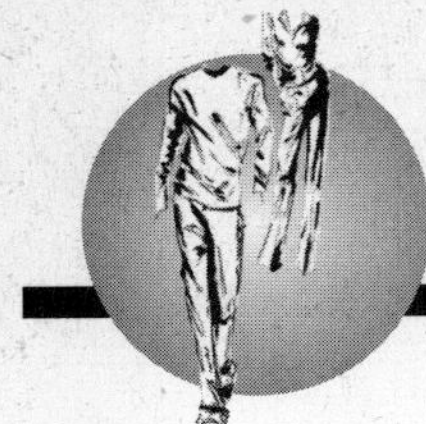

The Manufacturing Process

Directions: The steps in the manufacturing process are shown below. They are followed by a list of events that take place during the manufacturing steps. Decide when each event would occur and write the letter of that manufacturing step in the blank to the left of each number. Use each step only once.

Steps in the Manufacturing Process

A. Designing the line   **E.** Ordering materials   **I.** Assembling garments
B. Making samples   **F.** Creating production patterns   **J.** Finishing garments
C. Establishing costs   **G.** Creating layouts   **K.** Inspection
D. Taking orders   **H.** Cutting fabric   **L.** Distribution

---

_____ 1. Several hundred warm-up jackets must be returned to the line when it is found that they were made with defective zippers.

_____ 2. Using a computer, a worker decides that placing the pattern piece for a garment's collar in between the front and back pieces is the most efficient arrangement.

_____ 3. Sewers hand-stitch the buttons on the jacket of a men's suit.

_____ 4. A sewer replaces a notched collar with a chelsea collar as the designers rework their original idea.

_____ 5. A buyer selects two styles of women's wool coats for stores in British Columbia.

_____ 6. A manufacturer faxes a request for 300 square yards of a cotton paisley print from a textile converter in Durham, North Carolina.

_____ 7. After consulting a forecasting service, a stylist chooses subdued golds and grays for a new line of menswear.

_____ 8. A line worker and a supervisor solve a problem with a buttonhole sewer that feeds threads irregularly.

_____ 9. A loading dock supervisor signs a purchase order accepting delivery of a shipment of Hawaiian muumuus.

_____ 10. A wholesaler revises its price per garment when rising gasoline prices increase shipping expenses.

_____ 11. A worker checks the separate stacks of fabric pieces for the size 12 skirts to be sure that the correct bundles are ready to be moved from the area.

_____ 12. Working on a computer, an employee decides how to adapt the master pattern so the manufacturer can make garments in several sizes.

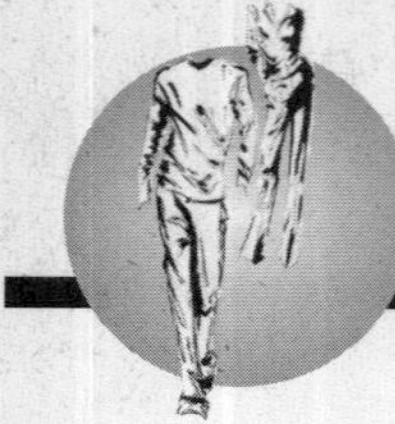

Fashion Promotion Strategies

Directions: Imagine that you work in fashion promotion for a large marketing firm that develops promotion strategies for clients. Some of your clients and their promotion needs are described below. For each client, decide the following: *a) what audience each promotion should target; b) what that audience needs to know; and c) what promotion methods would be most effective.* Write these decisions below, using ideas from the chapter and any others you may have.

1. A nationwide retailer needs to publicize an upcoming sale. _______________________

____

____

____

2. A textile company wants to promote a new fiber its research and development department has created.

____

____

____

____

____

3. A large garment manufacturer wants to publicize the first major clothing collection by a new designer.

____

____

____

____

4. A wool producers' association wants to promote wool products. _______________________

____

____

____

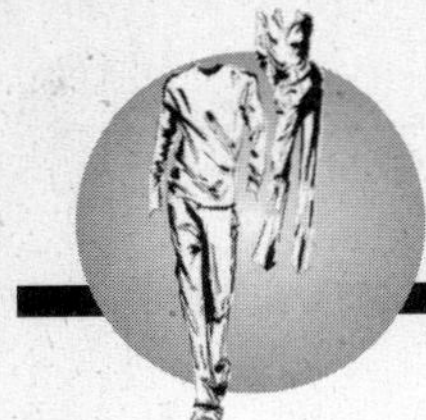

Is Apparel Production for You?

Part I. Directions: Read the feature on careers in apparel production on pages 150–153 in your textbook. The checklist below lists several qualities that a person desiring to work in the field of apparel production should possess. To find out whether you might be a good fit for this career field, place a check mark in the appropriate column for each quality.

Quality	Definitely	Mostly	Somewhat	Not at all
1. I pay attention to detail.				
2. I appreciate the way parts of a process fit together.				
3. I take pride in doing quality work.				
4. I am confident about giving my input on a project.				
5. I enjoy learning new skills.				
6. I believe that even small tasks are important.				
7. I have a talent for helping people work well as a group.				

Part II. Directions: Below are some skills a person desiring to work in the field of apparel production should possess. Evaluate your own skills by giving one example of how you demonstrate each skill.

8. Hand-eye coordination: ____

9. Mental concentration: ____

10. Communication: ____

11. Teamwork: ____

12. Flexibility: ____

13. Computer skills: ____

14. Based on this self-evaluation of your qualities and skills, do you have what it takes to make a career in apparel production? What qualities and skills would you need to develop that you do not yet possess? Do you think this field would interest you? Why or why not?

____

____

____

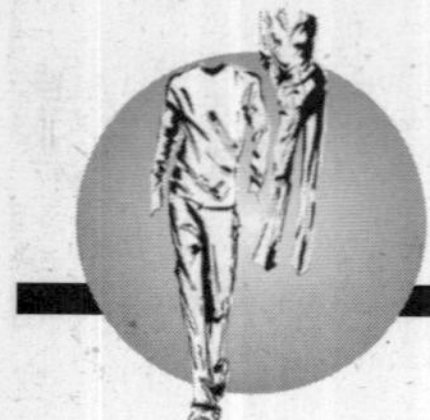

Constructing a Chronological Résumé

Part I. Directions: Imagine that you are interested in a position in apparel production and want a résumé that will convince employers to call you for an interview. A résumé summarizes your education, work experience, accomplishments, and skills. One type of résumé is called a *chronological résumé*. Read the guidelines below that explain what a chronological résumé is and how to construct one. Then complete the Part II activity below.

What Is a Chronological Résumé?

A chronological résumé emphasizes your employment history, beginning with the most recent position and working backwards. This type of résumé works well for workers who have followed a typical career path and who are seeking a position related to their past experience.

What Does It Include?

Name and contact information: At the top of your résumé, clearly identify your name, address, phone number where you can be reached during business hours, and e-mail address.

Job objective: This is an optional section. Write a brief statement of the type of position you are looking for. Avoid vague statements, such as "To use my skills in apparel production" or "To find a challenging job that will allow me to advance."

Education/training: For entry-level job seekers, this section should come before work experience. (If you had full-time work experience in the field in which you were applying, you would put the work experience section before the education section.) List the name of your high school, expected graduation date, and any relevant courses. (If you had education/training beyond a high school diploma, you would list that first and work backwards, including degrees, certificates, and diplomas.)

Work experience: List any jobs you have held, particularly those relevant to the type of job you are applying for. For each job, give the job title, name and location of employer, dates of employment, and duties and major accomplishments. Begin with your most recent position and work backwards.

Volunteer work: This is a useful section if you have not had much paid work experience and if your volunteer positions are relevant to the type of job you are applying for. Use the same format as for the work experience section.

Special skills: You may wish to list additional skills you have acquired that are not specified in your work experience section, such as computer, leadership, or communication skills.

Honors, awards: List any honors and awards you have received, particularly if they have some relevance to the job you are applying for.

Other Things to Remember

- Keep your résumé uncluttered and easy to read. Avoid small type and hard-to-read fonts.
- New job seekers should keep the résumé to one page.
- Use high-quality paper in a neutral color, such as white or off-white.
- Do not include information that is not relevant to the position, such as age or hobbies.
- Do not include the phrase "References available on request." This is assumed by employers.
- Avoid giving any negative information, but never exaggerate or lie on your résumé.
- Double-check spelling, grammar, and punctuation. Have someone else proofread it, if possible.
- Always include a cover letter with your résumé.

Part II. Directions: After reading the guidelines above, use word-processing software to keyboard a chronological résumé for an employer in the field of apparel production. Attach your résumé to this activity sheet.

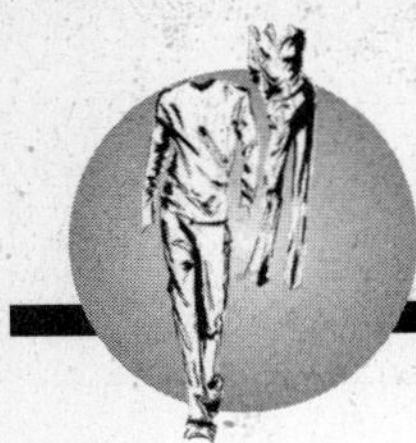

Understanding Color

Directions: As you read the chapter, answer the following questions. Later you can use this study guide to review for the Chapter 9 test.

1. What different effects can you achieve by using colors in your wardrobe? _______________________________

____

____

2. Why are blues and greens popular colors for summer clothes? _______________________________

____

3. How do warm and cool colors give illusions of movement? _______________________________

____

____

4. How can warm colors affect mood? _______________________________

____

5. How did Sir Isaac Newton contribute to the study of color? _______________________________

____

6. What is a pigment? _______________________________

____

7. How is the color wheel a useful tool for working with color? _______________________________

____

____

8. What are the three primary colors? _______________________________

____

9. Why is violet called a secondary color? _______________________________

____

(continued on next page)

Chapter 9
Study Guide (continued)

10. Contrast intermediate and complementary colors. Give an example of each. ________________

____

____

11. How do you change a color's value? ____

12. What is the technical name for a pastel? ____

13. What is intensity? What determines a color's intensity? _______________________________

____

14. How can you reduce the intensity of a color? _______________________________________

____

15. How can you see black and white if they aren't true colors? ____________________________

____

16. What should you remember about using an analogous color sheme? _____________________

____

17. Why are split-complementary color schemes easier to work with than complementary schemes? ________

____

18. What is a triadic color scheme? Give an example? ___________________________________

____

19. How is an accented neutral scheme used? ____

____

20. What three factors help determine the colors that best suit you? _______________________

____

21. When choosing personal colors for you, what should your main goal be?__________________

____

22. How can you dress to add height to your appearance? To diminish height? ________________

____

____

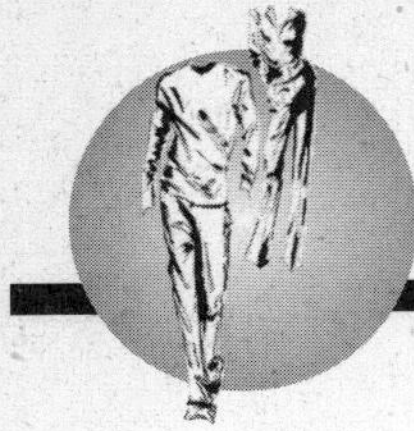

Creating a Color Wheel

Directions: Mix your own colors to complete the color wheel below. Use watercolors, pastels, colored pencils, or another medium of your choice. Experiment on another sheet of paper first. After your color wheel is complete, fill in the chart on page 46 with the correct color names.

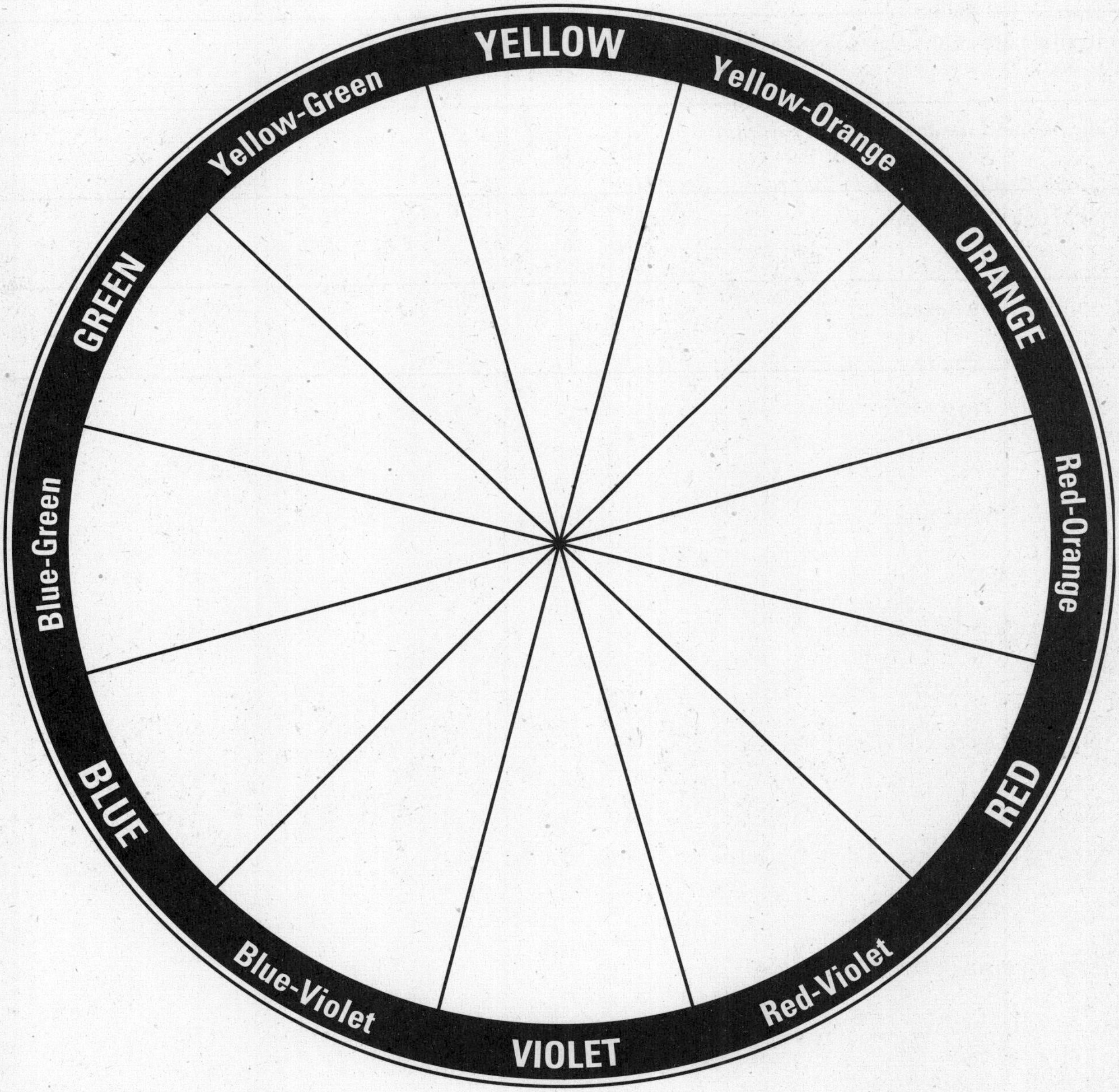

(continued on next page)

Clothing: Fashion, Fabrics & Construction Student Activity Manual
Copyright © by The McGraw-Hill Companies, Inc. All rights reserved.

Chapter 9
Activity (continued)

Terms	Colors
Primary colors (three colors)	
Secondary colors (three colors)	
Intermediate colors (six colors)	
Complementary colors (one example)	
Warm color (one example)	
Cool color (one example)	

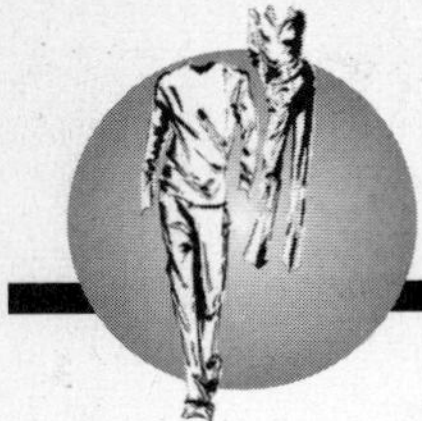

Color Schemes

Directions: On separate paper, prepare one example of each of the six color schemes on this page, using any of the methods listed below. Then answer the questions that follow.

- In a catalog or magazine, find a photo of an outfit with a specific color scheme. Cut and mount the photo on paper.
- Mount on paper a sample of a print, plaid, or striped fabric that demonstrates a color scheme.
- Sketch an outfit or fabric design. Color it with water colors, markers, or colored pencils.
- Describe in detail an outfit with the color scheme you want to show.
- Attach all of the above to this activity sheet and submit it to your teacher.

1. **Monochromatic.** In the color scheme you selected, how does the amount of contrast make a difference in the overall effect?

____

____

2. **Analogous.** Do the colors in your example blend well? Why or why not? _______________

____

____

3. **Complementary.** What can happen when two bright complements are used together? _______________

____

____

4. **Split-Complementary.** How does this color scheme compare to a complementary color scheme? _______

____

____

5. **Triadic.** What types of colors are easiest to wear when this color scheme is used? _______________

____

____

6. **Accented Neutral.** How does an accent color function in this color scheme? _______________

____

____

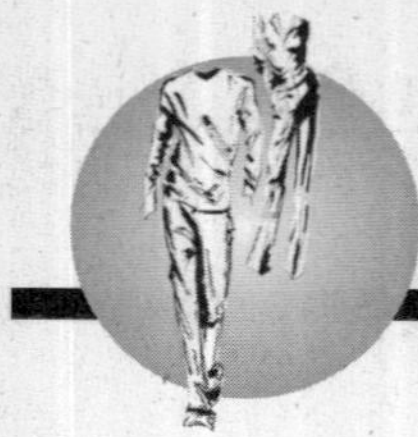

Colors for You

Directions: What colors make you look and feel your best? Follow the procedures below to discover your color preferences and flattering colors for you. A partner can help.

1. **What is your color personality?** Fill in the chart and study your responses.

Description	Color(s)
Your favorite color(s) in general	
Color(s) you liked wearing when you were younger	
Color(s) of your favorite clothing today	
Color(s) you last wore when receiving a compliment	
Color(s) that make you feel self-confident and attractive	
Color type you prefer: soft and light; bright and vivid; deep and muted; or rich and dark	

2. **How would you describe your hair, skin, and eyes?** Look closely at yourself in good natural light. Then circle the descriptive words that apply to you.

Hair		Skin		Eyes	
black	gray-blonde	cocoa-brown	peach	brownish-black	green
dark-brown	red	golden-brown	beige	brown	hazel
golden-brown	blonde	copper	ivory	amber	blue
reddish-brown	other	olive	white	gray	other
reddish-blonde		rosy	other		

3. **What is your skin undertone?** Your skin has one of two underlying skin tones, golden or bluish, which can influence how colors look on you. Examine your wrist and palm to determine skin undertone.

Golden _________   Bluish _________

4. **What colors look good on you?** To find out, cover your clothes with a white shirt or sheet and sit in a place with good natural lighting. Hold up clothing or fabric of different colors near your face. What are the effects on your skin, hair, and eyes?

Best Colors on You	Wearable Colors, But Not Best	Least Flattering Colors

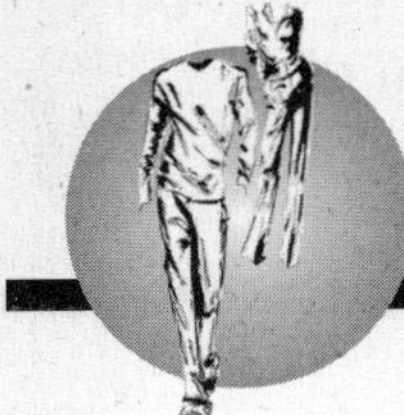

Choosing Wardrobe Colors

Directions: Planning your wardrobe around a few basic colors simplifies your shopping and makes your wardrobe more versatile. Learn here how to choose and use your basic colors.

1. **What basic colors would be good for you?** Fill in the chart. Then circle the two or three colors that appear most often and that you like. These can be your basic colors.

Description	Color(s)
Most common colors in your wardrobe	
Common colors in your wardrobe that match most easily with other colors	
Most flattering colors on you	

2. **What coordinating colors would be suitable?** Fill in the chart. Use the results for ideas as you plan outfits.

Description	Color(s)
Other colors that go well with my basic colors	
Colors that are closely related to my basic colors	
Colors that contrast with my basic colors	
Neutral colors that go well with my basic colors and with many other colors	

3. **How can you use your basic and coordinating colors?** Select a basic garment that you already own in one of your core colors (such as a blazer or a pair of pants). Using this garment and others in your wardrobe, plan outfits based on the color schemes below. Include accessories, such as belts and shoes. Describe the outfits on another sheet of paper. Knowing how to use your basic colors can help you focus on the best colors to choose when you add to your wardrobe.
   a. *Monochromatic:* use only values and intensities of the main color.
   b. *Analogous:* combine the main color with closely related colors.
   c. *Complementary:* combine the main color with the color across from it on the color wheel.
   d. *Accented neutral:* use black, white, or gray as the basis, brightened with a vivid color.

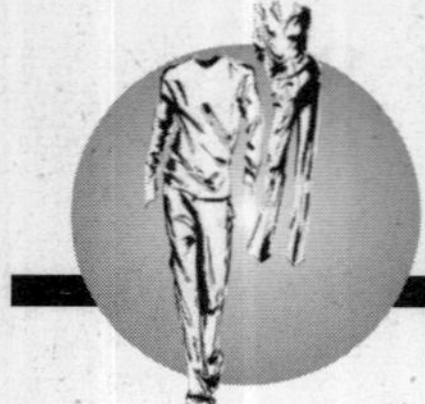

Solving Color Problems

Directions: Can you solve the color problems described here? Write answers that show your knowledge of color theory in the space provided.

1. This year I am making a special effort to wear "in" colors. I have been borrowing color ideas from friends I admire—the people who always look great. Why is that not working?

____

____

2. I would like to have broader shoulders. I have been working out, but progress is slow. In the meantime, are there any color tips that would help me get the look I want?

____

____

3. I have a closet full of clothes, but I can never find anything to wear. I try to buy clothes in many different colors, so finding things that go together should be easy. Am I doing something wrong?

____

____

4. People always tell me I look great in blue, and every time I get a present, it is another blue sweater or shirt. I have had it! Can I break out of my color rut, or am I stuck with blue for life?

____

____

5. I love bright colors, but right now I am fifteen pounds overweight. I have seen a doctor and started a diet. While I am dieting, should I stick to dull, dark colors?

____

____

6. I have noticed that on a dark and rainy day I end up wearing dark colors like gray and dark brown. Maybe I am on the wrong track. Should I dress to match my mood or to change it?

____

____

7. I would like to call attention to my best feature, my waistline. Is there a color trick I could use?

____

____

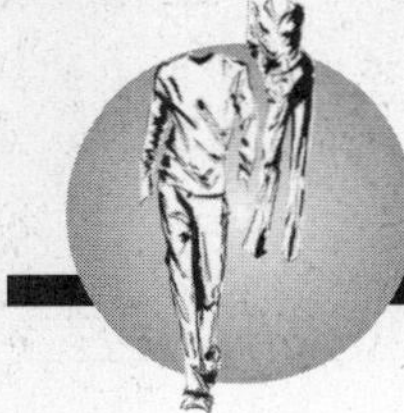

Understanding Design

Directions: As you read the chapter, answer the following questions. Later you can use this study guide to review for the test for Chapter 10.

1. What two areas of the body are considered in size ratios? _______________________________

____

2. How does the appearance of the shoulders differ in the triangle shape compared to the rectangle shape?

____

____

3. List the five elements of design. ____

____

4. Why is line called the most essential design element? What are three types of lines? _______

____

5. Why would a scalloped hem seem out of place on a business suit? _______________________

____

____

6. Identify some ways that a garment's features create vertical and horizontal lines. ___________

____

____

____

7. Which of the basic shapes would a stretchy knit fabric probably create? Why? ____________

____

____

8. How can you use a bell shape to create illusions? ____________________________________

____

____

(continued on next page)

Chapter 10
Study Guide (continued)

9. What decisions concerning space affect a garment's design? _______________________

____

____

10. What is texture? What factors determine a fabric's texture? _______________________

____

11. How is a pattern created? ____

____

12. How are the principles of design related to the elements of design? _______________

____

13. Compare the effects of symmetry and asymmetry in design. _______________________

____

____

____

14. What is proportion? ____

____

15. How is personal size a factor when considering proportion? _______________________

____

16. How can emphasis be used in a garment or wardrobe? _____________________________

____

17. How does rhythm contribute to fashion design? Name three ways that rhythm is achieved. _______________

____

____

18. Describe how an outfit shows harmony. ____

____

____

____

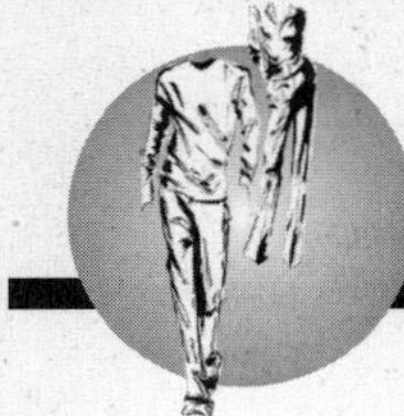

Design Opinions

Directions: Opinions on clothing design differ. Indicate your attitudes toward the statements below by using the scale below to rate each one. Then compare and discuss responses with the class. Write a summary of your discussion and attach it to this activity sheet.

Strongly Disagree 1	Disagree Somewhat 2	Neither Agree Nor Disagree 3	Agree Somewhat 4	Strongly Agree 5

______ 1. Shirts and blouses usually look best when tucked into pants or skirts.

______ 2. Straight-legged pants are more becoming than tapered pants and full-cut trousers.

______ 3. Overscale clothing, which is big, loose, and roomy, is attractive only on tall, thin people.

______ 4. Most people should pay more attention to proportion in their clothing.

______ 5. Skirt length should be determined by what looks best on an individual, not what is currently in style.

______ 6. Symmetrical clothing designs are usually more attractive than asymmetrical designs.

______ 7. Padded shoulders are attractive only on people with narrow or sloping shoulders.

______ 8. Tall people should never wear vertical stripes.

______ 9. Horizontal stripes tend to look better on males than on females.

______ 10. The accessories that complete an outfit should be kept simple.

______ 11. Big shirts look good on most people.

______ 12. Crisp fabrics make people look less slender than soft fabrics do.

______ 13. Small people should avoid large prints.

______ 14. Large people should avoid small prints.

______ 15. Shiny fabrics look best on slender people.

______ 16. Females can wear some colors that males cannot.

______ 17. How a garment looks on you is more important than how much you like it when choosing clothes.

______ 18. Females care more about clothing designs than males do.

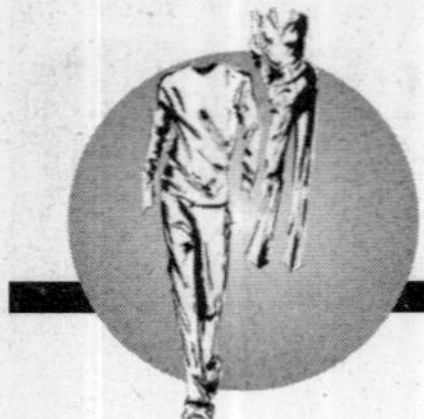

Analyzing Design

Directions: Look through magazine clothing advertisements to find an illustration of an especially attractive outfit. Cut and attach the illustration to separate paper and attach it to this activity sheet. Study the picture closely as you answer these questions about the outfit's design. What do you conclude about the outfit's overall design?

Elements and Principles of Design	Questions for Analysis	Your Observations and Analysis
Line	What line types and directions are present? What are their effects?	
Shape	Which of the shapes described in the text best fits the outfit?	
Space	How has space been handled in the design? Explain its effectiveness.	
Texture	Describe fabric textures in the outfit. Why were they used?	
Color	Describe the color(s). What is the effect?	
Balance	What type of balance is used in the outfit? Explain.	
Proportion	Are the parts of the outfit in balance? Explain.	
Emphasis	What is the focal point in the garment? Why is it noticeable?	
Rhythm	Is rhythm apparent in the design? If so, how?	
Harmony	Does the outfit show harmony? What accessories would (or do) promote harmony?	

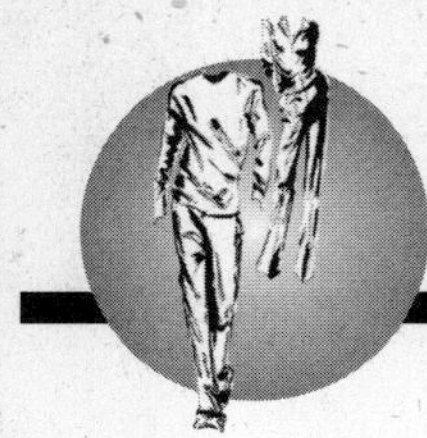

Fashion Design Solutions

Directions: The teens described below could use some fashion design advice. Can you help? For each teen suggest a more flattering outfit or a modification of the one worn. Explain why your suggestions would be more attractive on each person.

1. **Teen A.** This teen is a very tall, slender male. He wears a red and white running outfit with vertical stripes.

____

____

____

____

2. **Teen B.** Teen B is heavyset and has short legs. Her pants and matching shirt are made of soft, flowing fabric with a horizontally striped pattern in yellow and lavender. The gathered fabric falls from fitted yokes at her shoulders and hips.

____

____

____

____

3. **Teen C.** This teen wears an off-the-shoulder black knit dress with a jacket in a blue, green, and brown print. She wears dangling earrings and several bracelets and rings along with three strands of pearls. Her shoes are black patent with straps, open toes, and high heels.

____

____

____

____

4. **Teen E.** This teen is a tall, slender female. She wears a navy-blue dress with a tubular shape. It has a high neckline and hangs at mid-calf. She wears flat shoes and no accessories.

____

____

____

____

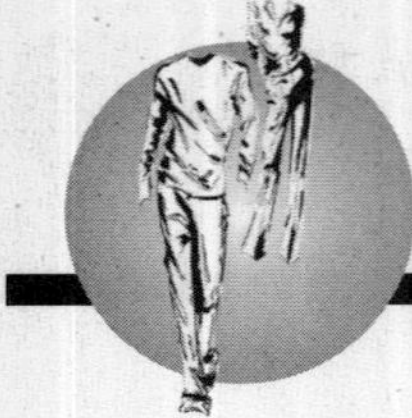

Design and Your Image

Directions: Experimenting with ways to change your appearance can be fun. You might be surprised to find different styles that look good on you. Select five ideas from the lists below or choose others. Then borrow clothing from family members or friends or visit clothing stores to find styles and fabrics to try. Write your evaluations and conclusions below. Consider the elements and principles of design as you experiment.

Looks to Try	boat neck	**Extras for Females**
big shirt	V neck	soft ruffles
knee-length shorts	vertical stripes	pleats
double-breasted jacket	horizontal stripes	culottes
sleeveless shirt	bright primary colors	raised waistline
shirt with contrasting collar	plaid	**Extras for Males**
checked fabric	bold print	knit shirt
nubby fabric	tweed	button-down collar
smooth, shiny fabric	corduroy	net shirt
terrycloth	velvet	shoulder tabs

Clothing Tried	Effect on Appearance

Conclusions

1. Is seeing yourself in styles that are not typical for you easy or difficult? Why? ________________

____

____

2. What new looks did you discover that you would like for your wardrobe? ________________

____

____

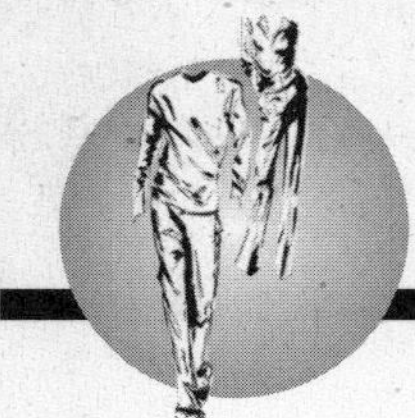

Is a Career in Design for You?

Part I. Directions: Read the feature on careers in design on pages 190–193 in your textbook. The checklist below lists several qualities that a person desiring to work in the field of design should possess. To find out whether you might be a good fit for this career field, place a check mark in the appropriate column for each quality.

Quality	Definitely	Mostly	Somewhat	Not at all
1. I like to shop for clothing.				
2. I like to read fashion magazines and articles.				
3. New fashion designs catch my eye.				
4. I have strong opinions about clothing styles.				
5. I notice the colors around me.				
6. I have a knack for putting outfits together.				
7. People often compliment me on my clothing.				
8. I enjoy working with fabric.				
9. I have a talent for sketching.				

Part II. Directions: Below are some skills a person desiring to work in the field of design should possess. Evaluate your own skills by giving one example of how you demonstrate each skill.

10. A "passion for fashion": ____

11. Communication: ____

12. Creativity: ____

13. Design knowledge: ____

14. Artistic ability: ____

15. Sewing skills: ____

16. Teamwork: ____

17. Strong work ethic: ____

18. Based on this self-evaluation of your qualities and skills, do you have what it takes to make a career in design? What qualities and skills would you need to develop that you do not yet possess? Do you think this field would interest you? Why or why not? Write your response on a separate sheet of paper and attach it to this activity.

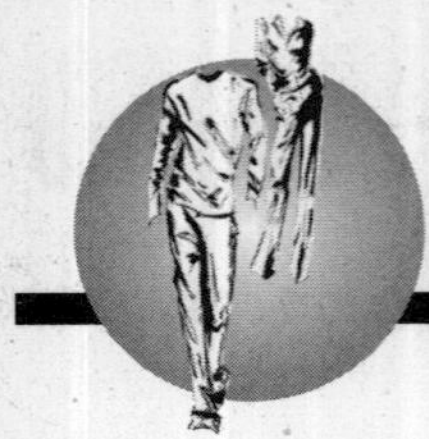

Career Achievements–
Looking Forward

Unit 3
Activity

Part I. Directions: To have a successful career, it is helpful to envision where you want to go and what you want to accomplish in your career. One way to do this is to imagine looking back on your career from a future point in time. For example, imagine that you have had a long, successful career in the design field (or a related field in fashion) and you are now receiving an award in recognition of your work and significant contributions to the field. Use the prompts below to outline what the person presenting you with the award might say about your career. Then write out the complete speech that you would want this person to give about your career. Write your speech on a separate sheet of paper and attach it to this activity.

1. How many years did you work in fashion? ____

2. How did you enter the fashion industry? Briefly describe your first job. ___________________

____

3. What other positions did you hold? ____

____

4. How is the fashion world different now than when you started out? _______________________

____

____

5. What significant changes or contributions did you bring to the world of fashion? What new products or process did you help bring about?

____

____

6. What do you regard as your greatest success in your career? ____________________________

____

____

7. Were there things you wanted to accomplish but did not? What were they, and what kept you from accomplishing them?

____

____

8. What advice would you give to those who are just starting out in the world of fashion? _______

____

Clothing: Fashion, Fabrics & Construction Student Activity Manual

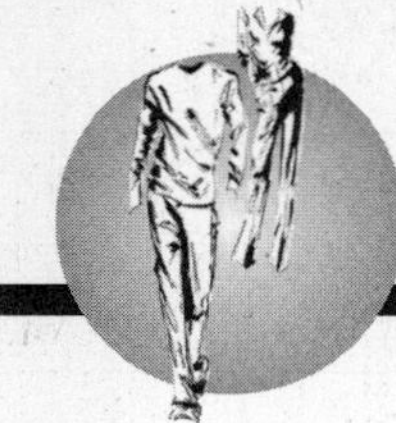

Textile Fibers

Directions: As you read the chapter, answer the following questions. Later you can use this study guide to review for the Chapter 11 test.

1. How are fibers turned into textiles? ____

____

2. Why don't natural fibers have a trade name? _______________________________________

____

3. Contrast tensile strength and resiliency. ____

____

4. Why is abrasion resistance an important quality in a fiber? _________________________

____

5. What is the difference between absorbency and wicking? ___________________________

____

____

6. How is cotton different in composition from wool? ________________________________

____

7. How does silk differ from all other natural fibers? ________________________________

____

8. According to Fig. 11-4, how do the care needs of cotton compare to those of silk? ______

____

____

9. What useful qualities does cotton supply in a garment? ____________________________

____

____

(continued on next page)

Clothing: Fashion, Fabrics & Construction Student Activity Manual

Chapter 11
Study Guide (continued)

10. What are some advantages of using flax in textiles?_______________________________________

____

11. What are silk's positive and negative qualities? ____

____

____

____

12. What happens during the spinning stage of fiber manufacturing?___________________________

____

13. What is a second- or third-generation fiber? ____

____

14. What positive qualities does rayon add to fabrics? _______________________________________

____

15. Name three positive traits and three negative traits of nylon. _____________________________

____

____

____

16. Compare and contrast acetate with triacetate. ____

____

____

17. Why are spandex and elastoester good choices for athletic wear? ___________________________

____

____

18. What is PLA fiber? Name three characteristics of PLA. ____________________________________

____

____

____

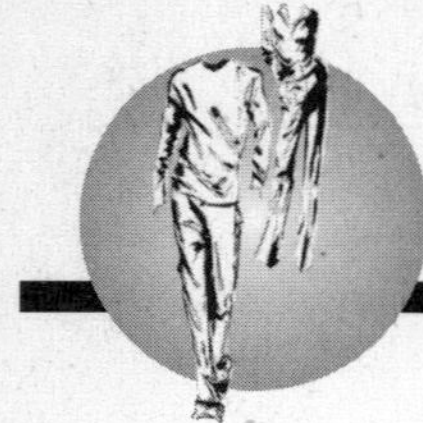

Fiber Characteristics

Directions: Each fiber has certain characteristics that influence the fabric's appearance and performance. The examples below indicate fiber characteristics described in the text. Fill in each blank with the fiber characteristic indicated. Some characteristics are used more than once.

_________________________ 1. The top of a shirt collar is frayed.

_________________________ 2. A beach towel is dripping wet after only one use.

_________________________ 3. A swimsuit stretches for a close fit.

_________________________ 4. Carpet indentations, made by a chair's legs, disappear when the chair is moved.

_________________________ 5. A jogging outfit makes you feel clammy while exercising.

_________________________ 6. The fabric on a garment rips when you make a sudden move.

_________________________ 7. A pair of pants has to be taken to the dry cleaner.

_________________________ 8. A shirt has many creases after wearing it for only an hour.

_________________________ 9. One brand of jeans lasts longer than others.

_________________________ 10. A pair of stretch pants is baggy in the knees after one wearing.

_________________________ 11. Tiny balls of fiber form on a sweater.

_________________________ 12. A shirt shines in the candlelight.

_________________________ 13. Certain dishtowels get soggy faster than others.

_________________________ 14. The thick pile on a fleece jacket stands back up after pressing it down with your hand.

_________________________ 15. The fabric on shirtsleeve elbows has worn thin.

_________________________ 16. A shirt looks good enough to wear when removed from the clothes dryer.

_________________________ 17. A pair of panty hose is baggy in the knees when worn.

_________________________ 18. Even active play does not ruin a child's overalls.

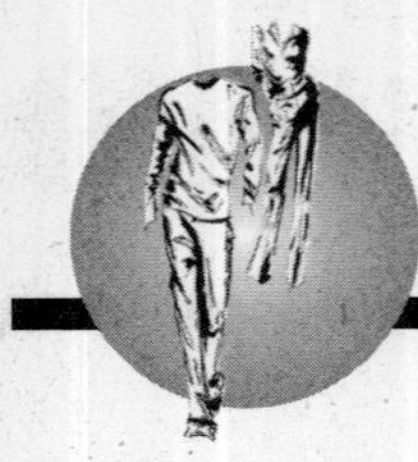

Studying Fibers

Directions: Collect a fabric sample for each fiber in the chart below. Refer to text pages 199 and 206 to review the fibers' characteristics. Then complete the chart as indicated.

Cotton	Wool	Rayon	Polyester
Step 1: Name the source of each fiber.			
Step 2: Pull a yarn or thread from each fabric sample. Untwist each yarn or thread to find one hairlike fiber. Look at the fiber under a microscope. Draw what you see.			
Step 3: Close your eyes and rub each piece of fabric on the inside of your arm. Describe how it feels.			
Step 4: Mount a small fabric sample for each fiber in the squares below.			
Step 5: Think about the characteristics of each fiber. Based on this information, suggest three possible uses for fabric made from the fiber.			

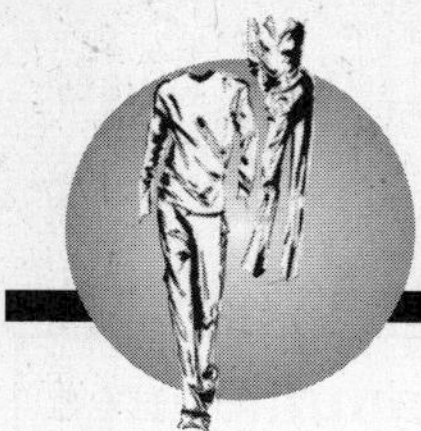

Fiber Classifications

Directions: Shown below and on the next page are some catalog descriptions of clothing and other fabric items. Look for fiber names in the descriptions. Write the trade names you find. Also list the names of any natural and manufactured fibers mentioned.

Catalog Description	Trade Names	Natural Fibers	Manufactured Fibers
Our thick Polartec® 200 polyester fleece blanket is as warm as wool without the weight. Cotton flannel sheets to match.			
Our own pullover sweater with three-button placket and polo collar. Imported, Ramie/cotton. Hand wash.			
Our hooded fleece pullover with front zipper has excellent wicking ability and is highly resistant to ultraviolet (UV) light. Especially suitable for mountain sports PLA/polyester. Washable.			
Made of an exclusive twill of moisture-wicking CoolMax® and smooth, breathable cotton, these pants will keep you feeling fresh and well dressed.			
With excellent stretchability and recovery, our exclusive skiwear continues to move with you after repeated stretching. 100% elastoester. Washable.			
Package of 6 pairs of athletic socks. Cotton/polyester/Lycra® spandex. Washable.			
Woven Fortrel®/polyester blouse looks and feels like silk—yet easy to care for and easy on your budget! Machine wash, tumble dry.			

(continued on next page)

Clothing: Fashion, Fabrics & Construction Student Activity Manual

Chapter 11
Activity *(continued)*

Catalog Description	Trade Names	Natural Fibers	Manufactured Fibers
Sleeveless sheath in polyester. Fully lined in acetate. Dry clean.			
Delicate floral embroidery softens this linen-like blouse of 100% woven rayon. Notched shirt collar and short sleeves with pretty scalloped embroidery.			
Two easy pieces in a supple, season-spanning Tencel® lyocell/rayon weave. Machine washable.			
Rug durably constructed with a blend of 66% polypropylene, 8% wool, 8% nylon, 8% rayon, 5% polyester, and 5% misc. fibers. Versatile and practical.			
This blend of Dacron® polyester and rayon wears very well and resists wrinkles even through a tough day on the job.			
Men's swim trunks with elasticized drawstring waist. A polyester/cotton/nylon blend in royal and white or red and white.			
Iridescent shantung blouse in 100% silk. Hand wash, line dry. Imported.			
These slimming trousers are unlined. 51% cotton/ 45% wool/4% Lycra® spandex. Dry clean. Imported.			
An affordable indulgence. Twinset sweaters in 100% cashmere from Inner Mongolia—the world's finest. Imported. Hand wash or dry clean.			
Our 100% olefin Berber carpet is strong and resists soil and mildew. Excellent for use in basement recreation rooms. Easily cleaned, dries quickly.			

Clothing: Fashion, Fabrics & Construction Student Activity Manual

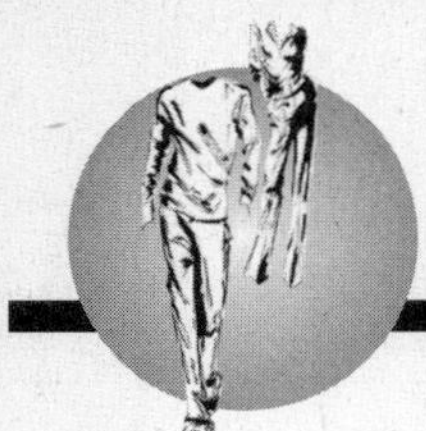

Fabric Construction

Directions: As you read the chapter, answer the following questions. Later you can use this study guide to review for the Chapter 12 test.

1. How are manufactured fibers turned into yarns? ____

____

2. How does the degree of twist affect a yarn's performance and appearance? _______________

____

3. How does texturing change the shape of filament yarns? _______________________________

____

4. What basic characteristics distinguish one fabric from another? ________________________

____

5. How can you judge a fabric's hand? ____

____

6. Which way do warp yarns run? Filling yarns? _______________________________________

____

7. What is the selvage on fabric? ____

____

8. Describe three type of grain in fabric. ____

____

9. What is a shuttle and what is its function? ____

____

10. How does a plain weave differ from a twill weave? ___________________________________

____

(continued on next page)

Chapter 12
Study Guide (continued)

11. What gives a satin weave its luster? ____

____

12. Name three functional qualities of "smart fabrics." _________________________________

____

13. What fabrics are made using the Jacquard weave? How are these fabrics used?___________

____

14. Why are knits comfortable to wear?____

____

15. Compare the advantages of using flat and circular knitting machines. __________________

____

____

16. What is the difference between a weft knit and a warp knit? __________________________

____

17. What is distinctive about raschel knits? ____

____

18. Why is felt called a nonwoven fabric? ____

____

19. List three characteristics of fleece fabrics. ____

____

____

20. What gives bonded fabrics added body? ____

____

____

21. How are quilted fabrics held together? ____

____

____

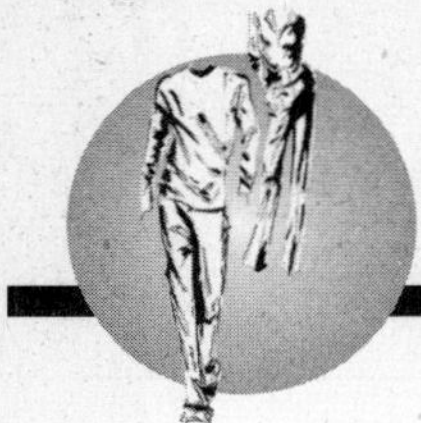

A Fabric Library

Directions: A fabric library is a collection of fabric samples. With a fabric library, you can easily reference many different fabrics to study and compare. You can begin a fabric library of your own with this two-page activity. Collect three fabric samples from the list of fabric constructions below. Mount the samples in the spaces provided, attaching them only at the top so the fabric undersides can be viewed. Then fill in the information about each sample. You can add to your library on your own.

Types of Fabric Construction

Plain weave	Plain weft knit
Twill weave	Purl knit
Satin weave	Rib knit
Pile weave with uncut loops	Double knit
Pile weave with cut loops	Warp knit
Figure weave	Nonwoven fabric

Fabric Sample #1 ____

Fabric name:_______________________

Fiber name:_______________________

Description of construction: ____

____

Uses for fabric:____

____

Care for fabric: ____

____

(continued on next page)

Chapter 12
Activity *(continued)*

Fabric Sample #2 ____

Fabric name: _______________________

Fiber name: _______________________

Description of construction: ____

____

Uses for fabric: ____

____

Care for fabric: ____

____

Fabric Sample #3 ____

Fabric name: _______________________

Fiber name: _______________________

Description of construction: ____

____

Uses for fabric: ____

____

Care for fabric: ____

____

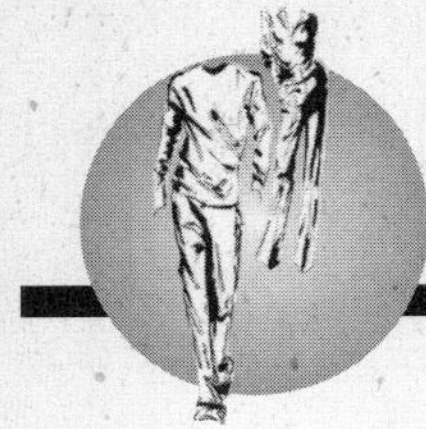

Fabric Finishes

Directions: As you read the chapter, answer the following questions. Later you can use this study guide to review for the Chapter 13 test.

1. What are fabric finishes? Why are finishes added to fabrics? _______________________________

____

____

2. Name the five methods of fabric dyeing. ____

____

3. How is color added in solution dyeing? ____

____

4. Which dyeing method adds color the latest in the clothes-making process? ____________________

____

5. Define colorfast. ____

____

6. How does a fabric's intended use affect the dye the manufacturer chooses? ____________________

____

____

7. What are the four most common methods of textile printing? _______________________________

____

8. How are rollers used in industrial textile printing?_______________________________________

____

____

9. In heat-transfer printing, why must the design on the pattern be reversed? ____________________

____

____

(continued on next page)

Chapter 13
Study Guide (continued)

10. What are the benefits of applying a texture finish? Name at least three feature finishes. ________________

____

____

11. How is calendering used to produce a moiré finish? __________________________________

____

____

12. What is meant by sizing a fabric? ____

____

13. What can you do to help maintain a fabric's performance finish? ________________________

____

____

14. What are the benefits of applying an antiseptic finish? ________________________________

____

____

15. Why is durable press a more accurate term than permanent press? ______________________

____

____

16. What does a shrink-resistant finish guarantee? _____________________________________

____

____

17. What is the benefit of a soil-release finish?_______________________________________

____

____

18. What is the difference between waterproof and water-repellent fabrics? __________________

____

____

Identifying Fabric Finishes

Directions: Each of the situations below relates to a fabric finish. Read the descriptions and write the name of the fabric performance finish in the space provided.

1. You dash through the rain across the parking lot and into the school. Water pools at your feet as the rain runs down the sleeves of your jacket. You can feel the dampness, however, as water starts to soak into the shoulders and across the back.	**2.** A classmate is modeling a new jogging outfit. You remark on how well it fits. Your classmate agrees: "Usually I buy them a little big since they shrink when I wash them, but the sales clerk said this is guaranteed not to shrink in the wash."
3. You are sharing a pizza with a friend. As your friend lifts a piece from the pan, a glob of melted cheese falls from the crust, dragging along a piece of sausage, and lands on the placemat. Quickly scooping up the oily spill, your friend says, "No problem. This will wash out."	**4.** As the weather starts to get cool, you decide to look into your fall wardrobe. Pulling out two wool sweaters from a storage box, you're dismayed to find that one has tiny holes eaten in the fabric. The other sweater, however, looks as good as when you put it away.
5. Your cousin is visiting for the weekend. You notice a pair of wrinkled slacks coming out of the suitcase, so you offer to get the iron. "That's okay," your cousin says. "The wrinkles come out after the pants hang in the closet for a few hours."	**6.** Your neighbor's five-year-old daughter is fascinated with her older sister's new velveteen vest. "Look," she says as she strokes the fabric up toward the neckline, then down toward the waist. "It's different."
7. An older relative asks you to make a pair of jeans for a child she looks after. "The problem is, he does not like new clothes. He says they are too stiff and scratchy." You assure her that you can buy soft denim fabric that won't bother him.	**8.** You notice your aunt's frustration at the family reunion. Every time she stands up, she reaches down to shake out her skirt to keep it from clinging to her legs and hips.

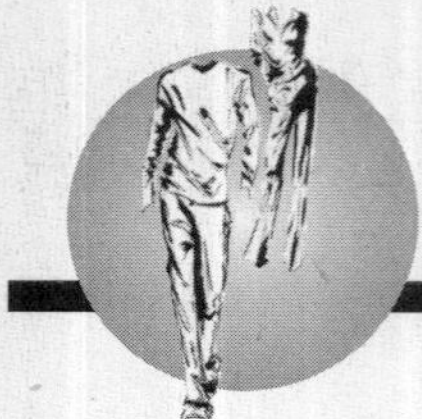

Fabric Finish Experiment

Directions: Some finishes make fabric care easier. Washable silk, for example, has been treated with a special finish, but how much difference does the finish make? Conduct this experiment to find out.

1. Cut two squares of washable, 100-percent silk and two of nonwashable, 100-percent silk.
2. Mount one square of each in the boxes labeled "Before."
3. Place the other two squares of fabric in warm (not hot) water for 10 minutes.
4. Remove the fabric squares and gently squeeze out the water. Hang the squares up to dry.
5. When the fabric has dried, press with an iron at a low temperature setting.
6. Mount the washed fabric squares in the boxes labeled "After."
7. Write the results of the experiment under "Conclusions" in the chart. Describe what happened to the size, texture, and appearance of each silk sample.

Washable Silk	Nonwashable Silk
B E F O R E	B E F O R E
A F T E R	A F T E R

Conclusions

Size: _______________________	Size: _______________________
Texture: _____________________	Texture: _____________________
Appearance: __________________	Appearance: __________________

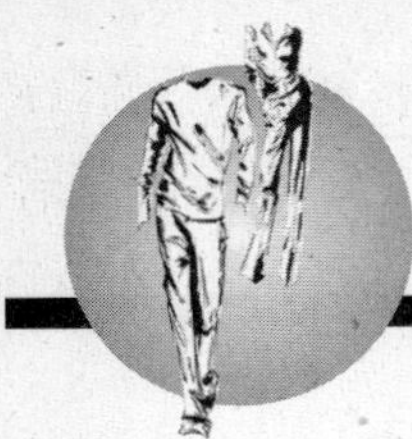

Is Textile Production for You?

Unit 4
Activity

Part II. Directions: Read the feature on careers in textile production, pages 244–247 in your textbook. The checklist below lists several qualities that a person desiring to work in the field of textile production should possess. To find out whether you might be a good fit for this career field, place a check mark in the appropriate column for each quality.

Quality	Definitely	Mostly	Somewhat	Not at all
1. I pay attention to detail.				
2. I am interested in the process by which things happen.				
3. I have a strong sense of self-direction.				
4. I like to take charge of my environment.				
5. I enjoy seeing how my efforts contribute to a group's success.				
6. I can balance several tasks at once.				

Part II. Directions: Below are some skills a person desiring to work in the field of textile production should possess. Evaluate your own skills by giving one example of how you demonstrate each skill.

7. Problem solving: ____

8. Analytical thinking: ____

9. Communication: ____

10. Teamwork: ____

11. Eye-hand coordination: ____

12. Record keeping: ____

13. Attention to detail: ____

14. Based on this self-evaluation of your qualities and skills, do you have what it takes to make a career in textile production? What qualities and skills would you need to develop that you do not yet possess? Do you think this field would interest you? Why or why not? Write your answers in the following space. If necessary, use an additional sheet of paper and attach it to this activity.

____

____

____

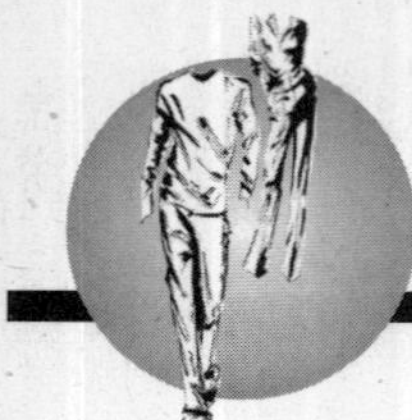

Career Paths in Textile Production

Part I. Directions: Imagine that you desire a career in textile production, perhaps as a textile chemist or a product engineer. Your chosen career will likely require some combination of education, training, and experience, along with a series of career moves that will lead to your ultimate goal. Choose and research a career in the textile production industry that interests you (see the information in your textbook for career ideas). Then use the information you gain to fill in the following.

1. Textile Production career goal: ____

2. Education needed: ____

   ____

   ____

3. Training/experience required: ____

   ____

   ____

4. Fill in the diagram below to indicate the career path you might take to arrive at your target job in textile production. Each line should indicate a job or career in your career path. Use as many or as few answer blanks as appropriate.

   ____________________ ➜ ____________________ ➜ ____________________ ➜ ____________________

5. List three things you could do now to prepare for this career.

   ____

   ____

   ____

   ____

6. List at least three sources you can use to learn more about this career and career path.

   ____

   ____

   ____

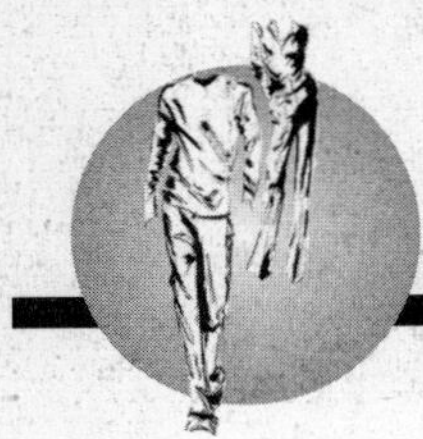

Clothing Care Basics

Directions: As you read the chapter, answer the following questions. Later you can use this study guide to review for the Chapter 14 test.

1. How can taking time to care for clothing save time later? ___________________________________

____

____

2. Explain two ways that giving clothes needed care can save you money. ______________________

____

3. What are enzymes? How do they work? ____

____

4. What can happen if you launder a garment without treating any stains? ____________________

____

5. List at least four basic methods of treating stains before laundering. ______________________

____

____

6. What may happen if you use an enzyme presoak on a silk shirt? Why? ______________________

____

7. Describe two ways to treat stains with detergent just before laundering. ____________________

____

____

8. Give some suggestions for using a prewash soil-and-stain remover. ________________________

____

____

____

(continued on next page)

Chapter 14
Study Guide (continued)

9. What steps would you take to hang a linen suit jacket? ____________________________

____

____

10. What would you tell a friend who starts to hang a hand-knitted sweater in the closet? ______________

____

____

11. What factors determine the instructions printed on a garment's care label? ______________

____

____

12. What can you assume if a garment care label doesn't include ironing instructions? ______________

____

13. List the six basic fabric care symbols. ____

____

____

14. What does an X through a care label symbol mean? ______________________________

____

15. How can you use shelves to organize clothes?___________________________________

____

____

____

16. Explain how to store clothes for a season. _____________________________________

____

____

____

Clothing: Fashion, Fabrics & Construction Student Activity Manual

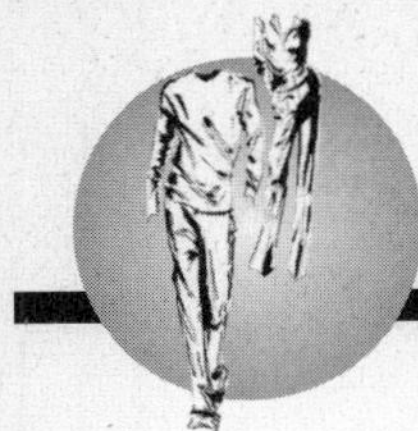

Stain Removal Experiment

Directions: When fabric becomes stained, do you know what to do? Practice by conducting this experiment.

1. Cut eight small fabric samples that will fit the chart on the next page. Use one fabric for all samples. Your classmates should use different fabrics.
2. Stain two of the samples with ballpoint ink, two with chocolate, two with chewing gum, and two with a soft drink.
3. After the stains have dried, mount one sample of each stain in the spaces labeled "Before on page 78".
4. Follow the stain removal directions on text pages 254-55 to remove the stains from the remaining samples.
5. Mount the treated, dry samples in the spaces labeled "After" on page 78.
6. Record your observations and conclusions below.

Observations

1. Describe each stain after the removal process.

   Ink: ____

   Chocolate: ____

   Gum: ____

   Soft drink: ____

2. Which stain was easiest to remove?_________________________________

3. Which stain was most difficult to remove? __________________________

4. Did any stain require more than one treatment? Explain. _______________

   ____

Conclusions

5. How successful were you at removing the stains?______________________

   ____

   ____

6. Compare your results to those of classmates. Do you think the type of fiber or fabric is related to successful stain removal? Explain.

   ____

   ____

(continued on next page)

Chapter 14
Activity (continued)

Ballpoint Ink Stain	Chocolate Stain
B E F O R E	B E F O R E
A F T E R	A F T E R

Chewing Gum Stain	Soft Drink Stain
B E F O R E	B E F O R E
A F T E R	A F T E R

Clothing: Fashion, Fabrics & Construction Student Activity Manual

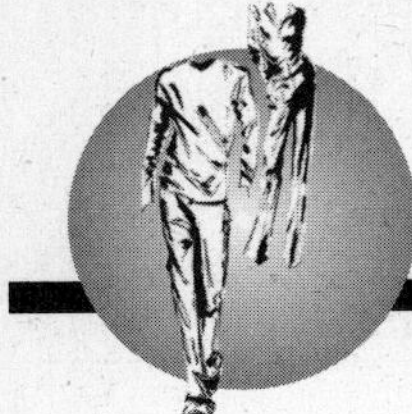

Laundry and Dry Cleaning

Directions: As you read the chapter, answer the following questions. Later you can use this study guide to review for the Chapter 15 test.

1. What important information do you find on laundry product labels? _______________________________
____

2. What do detergents do? ____

3. List six basic varieties of detergent. ____
____

4. Describe one advantage and one disadvantage of using nonchlorine bleach. _______________________
____

5. Why should bleach be diluted with water before making contact with clothes? ______________________
____

6. Describe two ways to add fabric softener. ____
____

7. How do dye-trapping sheets work in the washer? ____
____

8. Name four basic pieces of laundry equipment. ____

9. How do washing machines help you customize laundering to each load of laundry? __________________
____
____

10. What is the benefit of the newer high-efficiency washing machines? ____________________________
____

11. What is the purpose of an ironing board pad and cover? _____________________________________
____

(continued on next page)

Chapter 15
Study Guide (continued)

12. How and why should clothes be separated by color for laundering? _________________________

____

____

13. Give three suggestions for separating and washing clothes by fabric._________________________

____

____

____

14. What may happen if you don't check the pockets before laundering a garment? _________________

____

15. What three basic temperature settings do washing machines offer? When is each one recommended?

____

____

16. How can you treat stains when hand washing delicate fabrics? _____________________________

____

17. Why should you clean the lint filter in the dryer after each load? ___________________________

____

18. Give three suggestions for line-drying clothes. ____

____

____

____

19. What temperature setting should you choose for ironing a blended-fiber fabric? _______________

____

20. What things should you mention to a dry cleaner when bringing in clothes for cleaning? _________

____

Clothing: Fashion, Fabrics & Construction Student Activity Manual

Comparing Costs

Directions: With many laundry products available in a variety of forms and sizes, getting the best value can be a challenge. Answer the questions below to practice your "shopping savvy." Use the following formula to calculate price per ounce: *Cost per ounce = price ÷ number of ounces.* Round answers up or down to the nearest cent.

> **Zippy Mart Groceries carries two sizes of your usual brand of laundry detergent, Diamond Powder (DP), in 73-ounce and 87-ounce boxes. A 68-ounce box of Crystal Concentrated (CC) detergent is also available.**

____________ 1. What is the price per ounce of the 73-ounce box of Diamond Powder that is on special for $5.89?

____________ 2. What is the price per ounce of the 87-ounce box of Diamond Powder for $8.59?

____________ 3. Between the 73-ounce and 87-ounce boxes, which is the better buy?

____________ 4. On the larger size of Diamond Powder you see a peel-off coupon for 75¢ off. What is the price per ounce of the 87-ounce size with the coupon?

____________ 5. Which size is the better buy if the coupon is used?

____________ 6. At $10.56, what does Crystal Concentrated detergent cost per ounce?

____________ 7. The Crystal brand is a concentrated powder. The label says you need only ⅓ as much as a regular powder. If the label recommends you use 2 ounces of Crystal Concentrated per load, how much Diamond Powder would it take to do a load of wash?

8. You can also compare detergents according to cost per load of laundry. In the chart below, enter the price per ounce that you've already determined for each detergent. (Use the coupon.) Then enter the number of ounces of each product needed to wash a load of laundry. (See question 7.) Next, multiply the price per ounce by ounces per load to find the cost per load. Finally, compare the cost per load of all the detergents. In the last column of the chart, rank the detergents according to which is the best value. Use number 1 for the best value.

Box Size	Price Per Ounce	Ounces Per Load	Cost Per Load	Value Ranking
73-oz. DP	a.	b.	c.	d.
87-oz. DP	e.	f.	g.	h.
68-oz. CC	i.	j.	k.	l.

9. What can you conclude about the relationship between price and value? _______________

____

____

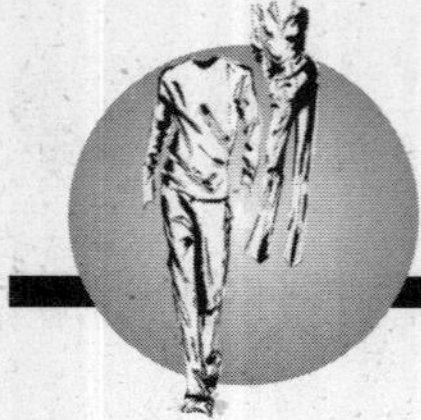

Laundry Advice

Directions: Imagine that you're filling in for the regular on-line customer service representative at a county cooperative extension Web site. You receive the following e-mails asking for answers to laundry questions. Write your reply to each one in the space provided, using information in the chapter to guide your advice.

1. "I took some spare cotton sheets out of storage for a relative's visit. They smell a little musty. How can I get rid of the odor?"

____

____

2. "Many of our children's classmates are coming down with coughs and colds. Is there some way to treat my kids' clothes to help kill the germs they pick up from sick friends?"

____

____

3. "My white clothes come out of the wash gray and dingy. Is there any way to avoid this?" _______________

____

____

4. "I think my dryer puts wrinkles in my clothes. At least, they always need ironing when I machine-dry them."

____

____

____

5. "I used a home dry cleaning kit on some clothes labeled 'Dry-clean only,' but some of the stains didn't come out. I followed the directions exactly. Is the kit defective?"

____

____

6. "Some of my clothes feel itchy the first time I wear them after washing them. Is there something I can do about that?"

____

____

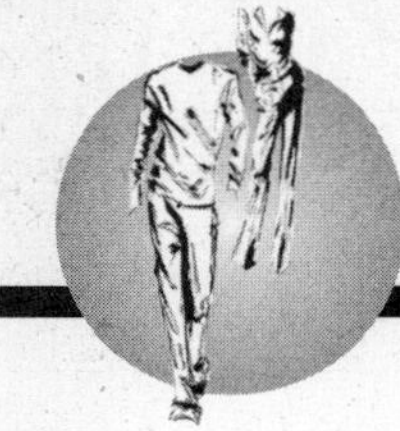

Redesign, Repair, and Recycle

Directions: As you read the chapter, answer the following questions. Later you can use this study guide to review for the Chapter 16 test.

1. Describe at least three ways you might redesign a garment to update its look. ________________________
____
____
____

2. Give a short explanation of how to shorten a hem. ____
____
____
____

3. How can you make minor adjustments in a garment's width? ________________________________
____
____

4. Suggest ways to "dress up" a garment for a more formal look. ______________________________
____
____
____

5. What may result from skipping steps when using a commercial dye on clothing?_______________
____
____

6. What can you do if you can't find a match for a button that needs replacing? ________________
____
____

(continued on next page)

Chapter 16
Study Guide (continued)

7. What is a drawback to mending a tear with machine zigzag stitching? _______________________

____

____

8. Besides updating a style, how can decorative trim be used to extend the life of some garments? __________

____

____

9. What should you do if you don't have the time or tools to make a needed repair immediately? __________

____

____

10. How does recycling clothes help preserve the natural environment? ________________________

____

____

____

11. How can older garments find new wearers? ____

____

____

____

12. Why might children prefer a garment made from used fabric? _______________________________

____

13. What items can be made by patchwork? ____

____

14. What should you look for in fabric pieces to stitch together in a patchwork project? _______________

____

15. What would you do to a flannel shirt to make it more useful for household cleaning?_______________

____

____

     Clothing: Fashion, Fabrics & Construction Student Activity Manual

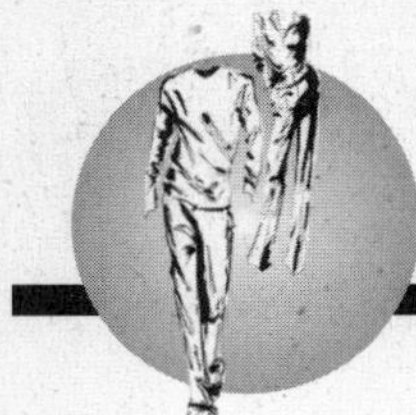

Fabric Dye Experiment

Directions: Conduct this experiment to determine how different fabrics absorb dye.

Equipment and Materials

- Three samples of white fabric: 100% cotton, 100% polyester, and a cotton/polyester blend
- Liquid or powdered fabric dye
- Water
- Container, such as a large bowl, pan, or sink
- Rubber gloves
- Paper towels
- Bleach or cleanser

Procedure

1. Protect your work area with old newspapers or paper towels. In the container, mix the fabric dye with water according to package directions.
2. Wearing rubber gloves, add the fabric samples to the dye solution. Stir constantly for 5 to 8 minutes (or follow package directions).
3. Rinse the samples according to package directions. Blot dry on paper towels.
4. Discard the dye solution and clean the container with bleach or cleanser.
5. Mount small samples below when dry. Complete the questions that follow.

100% Cotton Fabric	100% Polyester Fabric	Fabric Blend

Observations and Conclusions

1. Which sample absorbed the most dye? _____________________ The least dye? _______________

2. Summarize your findings. ____
   ____

3. Based on these findings, would dyeing be a worthwhile way to add or change the color of any garments in your wardrobe? Why or why not?
   ____
   ____

4. What are other ways to add color to garments? ___________________________________
   ____

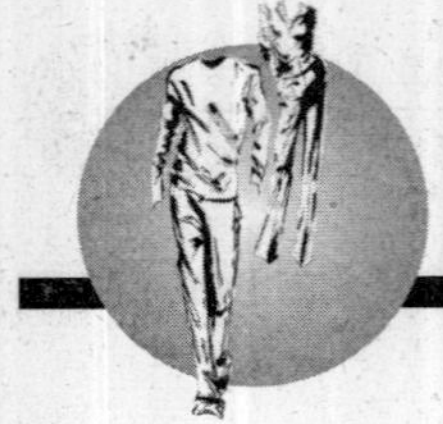

New Ideas for Clothes

Directions: In every closet are clothes that are one step away from uselessness—or usefulness. Suppose the items in the chart are yours. For each one, suggest two ways that the item can be given added life or a new use. Explain any updating or other changes, if needed.

Clothing Item	Idea #1	Idea #2
Exercise Wear An old exercise outfit is too worn to keep you warm on chilly morning runs, but it is soft and comfortable.		
Sweater A white sweater fits you physically, but it doesn't fit your changing style. You are just not a plain-white-sweater person anymore.		
Suit Jacket A particular suit jacket looks great and fits well, but it has always been too warm to wear with the rest of the outfit. It is practically brand new, but starting to look dated.		
Jeans A pair of faded jeans were fine for running errands or relaxing at home—until you missed the "Wet Paint" sign on a park bench. You no longer want to wear them with that green paint stain across the seat.		

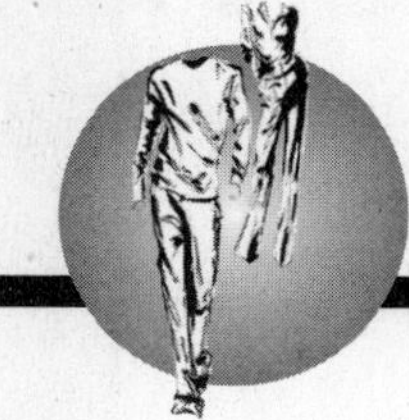

Is Fashion Services for You?

Part I. Directions: Read the feature on careers in fashion services on pages 296–299 in your textbook. The checklist below lists several qualities that a person desiring to work in the field of fashion services should possess. To find out whether you might be a good fit for this career field, place a check mark in the appropriate column for each quality.

Quality	Definitely	Mostly	Somewhat	Not at all
1. I am self-motivated.				
2. I am a good listener.				
3. I genuinely enjoy helping people.				
4. I am sensitive to people's needs and circumstances.				
5. I have confidence in my own judgment.				
6. My reputation is very important to me.				

Part II. Directions: Below are some skills a person desiring to work in the field of fashion services should possess. Evaluate your own skills by giving one example of how you demonstrate each skill.

7. Communication: ____

8. Organization: ____

9. Management: ____

10. Self-discipline: ____

11. Knowledge of fibers and fabrics: _________________________________

12. Sewing skills: ____

13. Fashion sense: ____

14. Based on this self-evaluation of your qualities and skills, do you have what it takes to make a career in fashion services? What qualities and skills would you need to develop that you do not yet possess? Do you think this field would interest you? Why or why not? Write your answers in the space provided. If necessary, use an additional sheet of paper and attach it to this activity.

____

____

____

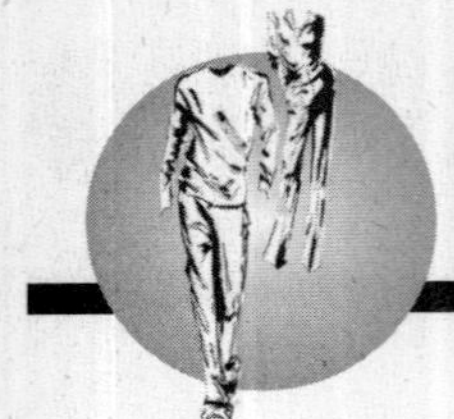

Constructing a Skills-Based Résumé

Part I. Directions: Imagine that you are interested in a position in fashion services and want a résumé that will convince employers to call you for an interview. A résumé summarizes your accomplishments, skills, education, and work experience. One type of résumé is called a skills-based résumé. Read the guidelines below that describe a skills-based résumé and how to construct one.

What Is a Skills-Based Résumé

A skills-based résumé emphasizes skill sets and accomplishments rather than job history, as in the chronological résumé. This type of résumé works well for new job seekers, career changers, and those with gaps in their employment history. The emphasis is on the skills you've acquired that would translate into the type of position you are now seeking.

What Does It Include?

Name and contact information: At the top of your résumé, clearly identify your name, address, phone number where you can be reached during business hours, and e-mail address.

Summary: Write a brief summary of your accomplishments and career objective.

Skills/accomplishments or areas of strength: This section should be broken into several headings that describe your most important skills, experience, or strengths. For instance, you might use "Sewing Skills" and "Computer Skills" as two headings. Under each heading, describe your skills and accomplishments in that area. Do not list any dates of employment or names of employers. This section can include volunteer work experience, but it should be clear that it is volunteer work. Honors or awards can also be mentioned here.

Education: List the name of your high school, expected graduation date, and any relevant courses. (If you had education/training beyond a high school diploma, you would list that first and work backwards, including degrees, certificates, and diplomas.)

Work history: In a "pure" skills-based résumé, no employers would be listed. However, since potential employers generally like to know where you have worked, you should add a work history section after the other sections that briefly states each job title, name and location of employer, and dates of employment

Other Things to Remember

- Keep your résumé uncluttered and easy to read. Avoid small type and hard-to-read fonts.
- New job seekers should keep the résumé to one page.
- Use high-quality paper in a neutral color, such as white or off-white.
- Do not include information that is not relevant to the position, such as age or hobbies.
- Avoid giving any negative information, but never exaggerate or lie on your résumé.
- Double-check spelling, grammar, and punctuation. Have someone else proofread it, if possible.
- Always include a cover letter with your résumé.

Part II. Directions: After reading the above guidelines, use word-processing software to keyboard a skills-based résumé for an employer in the field of fashion services. Attach your résumé to this activity sheet.

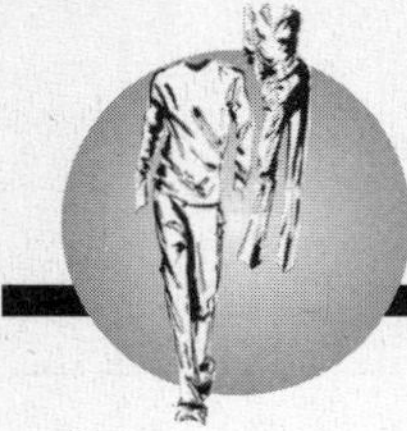

Exploring Options

Directions: As you read the chapter, answer the following questions. Later you can use this study guide to review for the test for Chapter 17.

1. Give a one-sentence summary of each of the five steps in evaluating a wardrobe. _____________

____

____

____

2. How is a wardrobe chart useful for taking a clothing inventory? _____________________________

____

3. What factors might you consider when deciding what to do with a garment? _________________

____

____

4. What helps distinguish wants from needs? Give an example of a reason for wanting a new garment. _______

____

____

5. What factors might help you decide whether to add a garment to your wardrobe? _______________

____

____

6. How is a wardrobe chart a useful tool for wardrobe evaluation? _________________________

____

____

(continued on next page)

Clothing: Fashion, Fabrics & Construction Student Activity Manual
Copyright © by The McGraw-Hill Companies, Inc. All rights reserved.

Chapter 17
Study Guide (continued)

7. List some resources for carrying out a wardrobe plan. ___________________________________

____

8. What are three basic options regarding a wardrobe plan when money is limited? _____________

____

9. What kinds of skills are especially helpful for meeting wardrobe needs when a budget is limited? _________

____

10. How can time be a resource for carrying out a wardrobe plan? ____________________________

____

11. How can you combine garments you already own to expand your wardrobe? _________________

____

12. Besides making and repairing clothing, how can you use sewing skills to save money? _________

____

13. Contrast department stores and specialty stores. _______________________________________

____

____

14. Why are clothes at off-price retailers lower priced than at department stores? _______________

____

____

15. Contrast thrift stores and consignment shops. ____

____

____

16. What are the advantages and disadvantages of on-line and catalog shopping? ________________

____

____

____

 Clothing: Fashion, Fabrics & Construction Student Activity Manual

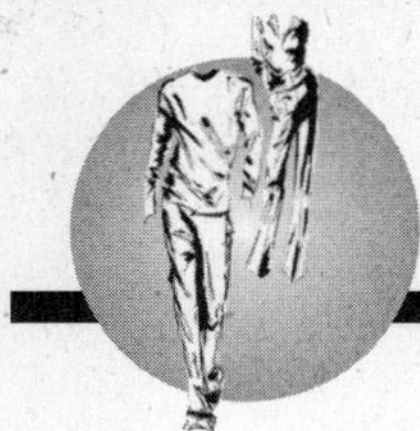

Taking a Wardrobe Inventory

Directions: Wardrobe planning begins with taking an inventory of what you currently own. Practice the inventory process below. Choose seven varied garments or accessories from your wardrobe, including some that you have had for a long time. List them in the left column of the chart. Then fill in the rest of the chart as indicated. Later, you could expand this to a complete inventory that includes all the garments in your wardrobe.

Description: Include color and style.

Evaluation: Note how you use the garment and its condition.

Action Plan: Note whether the garment should be kept, repaired, given away, discarded, or replaced. Explain what action will be taken.

Priority List: On a separate sheet of paper, create a prioritized list of items to buy or replace for those items that you eliminated from your wardrobe. Attach your list to this activity sheet.

Clothing	Description	Evaluation	Action Plan

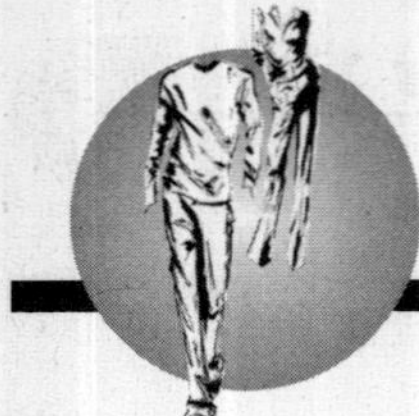

Evaluating Needs and Wants

Directions: What clothing and accessories have you thought about owning? List seven such items below. Then explain why you would like to have each item. Decide whether or not each item is a necessity and place a checkmark under need or want. Compare all the items and give each a priority number from 1 (most important to have) to 7 (least important to have). After you have taken a wardrobe inventory, this process helps you plan future additions.

Item	Why would you like to have this item?	Need?	Want?	Priority

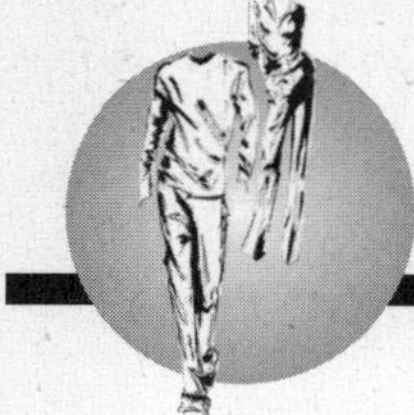

Expanding Your Wardrobe

Directions: With a little imagination, you can get more mileage from your wardrobe. Complete this activity to practice your creative thinking.

1. Listed below are garments that might be found in a wardrobe. Use them to create at least six attractive outfits.

khaki slacks   *navy crew-neck shirt*   *white dress shirt*
dark gray slacks   *yellow sweater*   *black vest*

____

____

____

____

____

2. Suggest two garments or accessories that would be very useful in expanding even further the ideas you had for question 1. Explain how you would use each of these additional items to create more new outfits.

____

____

____

____

____

3. Imagine that you want to give a certain look to a white, buttoned shirt. Suggest ways to achieve the looks described below. You may suggest ways to accessorize or to redesign the shirt.

a. *Sophisticated and professional*

____

____

____

(continued on next page)

Chapter 17
Activity *(continued)*

b. *"Country casual"*

____

____

____

c. *Festive and glittery*

____

____

____

4. Think of garments in your wardrobe that could be worn in combinations that you've never tried before. Describe three new outfit possibilities. _______________________________________

____

____

____

5. What single garment would make a versatile addition to your wardrobe? Explain how that item could be used in a variety of ways with garments you already own. _______________________

____

____

____

6. How can the ideas you've practiced in this activity help you save money? _______________________

____

____

____

Clothing: Fashion, Fabrics & Construction Student Activity Manual

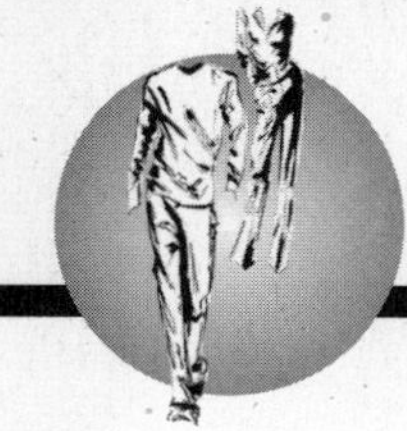

Accessing Information

Directions: As you read the chapter, answer the following questions. Later you can use this study guide to review for the Chapter 18 test.

1. List four major sources of information for clothing shoppers. _________________________________

____

2. Why are information ads useful to shoppers? ____

____

3. How do image ads try to make people want to buy a product? ___________________________________

____

____

4. Why do newspaper ads tend to be more informative than magazine ads? ___________________________

____

____

5. How do advertisers take advantage of the Internet? ____

____

____

6. How might designers use product placement to have their products used? _________________________

____

____

7. How can catalogs be useful, even if you don't buy from them? __________________________________

____

____

8. Why were clothing labels unnecessary at one time? ____

____

____

(continued on next page)

Chapter 18
Study Guide (continued)

9. Identify and describe two pieces of legislation that help consumers gather information about garments for sale.

____

____

____

____

____

10. List the five additional types of information that are mandatory on garment labels. ________________

____

____

11. List five pieces of information that you might find on a garment label. ________________________

____

12. What promises does a warranty often carry? ____

____

13. How are pre-season sales different from clearance sales? _______________________________

____

14. Name two ways to avoid impulse buying ____

____

____

15. How do overruns compare in quality with other garments sold at discounted prices? _____________

____

16. What two important facts does the label "as is" on a garment tell you? ____________________

____

____

17. Describe the different return policies that a store might follow. ____________________________

____

____

   Clothing: Fashion, Fabrics & Construction Student Activity Manual

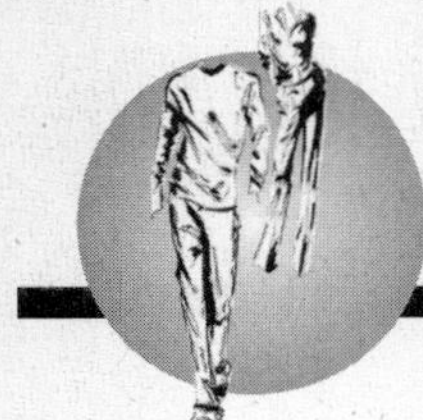

Advertising Appeals

Directions: Clever advertising can make clothing seem irresistible. After you buy, however, the pizzazz may disappear. Seeing through sales appeals can help you avoid such fashion mistakes. Study the sales appeals listed below and match them to the sample advertisements by writing the correct letters in the spaces at the left. Then identify one way to resist each type of advertising. Write your responses on a separate sheet of paper and attach it to this activity sheet.

> **A.** *Celebrity appeal:* buy this because a famous person does.
> **B.** *Bandwagon:* buy this because everybody else does.
> **C.** *Prestige:* buy this because it will bring you status.
> **D.** *Savings:* buy this because it is a bargain.
> **E.** *Novelty:* buy this because it is new.
> **F.** *Glittering generalities:* buy this because the statements sound positive (but meaningless).
> **G.** *Image making:* buy this because you will be entirely different if you do.

_____ 1. Winners like tennis star Stacy Wilson wear Slimshapers.

_____ 2. Capture that incredible dazzle, impossible until now: Lumino Separates.

_____ 3. Luxury recognized anywhere. You can tell it's Elongee. It costs more, but it's worth it.

_____ 4. Jump ahead of the crowd in trendsetting workout garb from our new spring collection.

_____ 5. Fabulous values just in time for Father's Day. Great looks for less.

_____ 6. Margaret Fielding Furs: exclusively for you; a tribute you deserve.

_____ 7. Everybody's falling in love with flowing, romantic dresses from Alice Clair.

_____ 8. Discover the delightful styling, the extraordinary impact, the perfection of Millside Manor shirts.

_____ 9. Be ahead of your time. Innovate with fresh new warm weather looks from L.P. Smith.

_____ 10. Transform yourself with Bravo Sportswear. Trade yesterday's drab looks for that Bravo Girl flair.

_____ 11. Don't be left out of the summer fun. Your friends know the secret: Warrenwear.

_____ 12. Bewitching, distracting—a new you in exotic Malamar designs.

_____ 13. Richard Cather has what it takes to be a star. And the classic good looks of Deland sports coats have the same star quality.

_____ 14. This week only at Binyan and Mackenzie's—10% to 15% off on all garments in our annual super sale.

_____ 15. Nothing makes you stand out from the rest more than fashions by Sharleen.

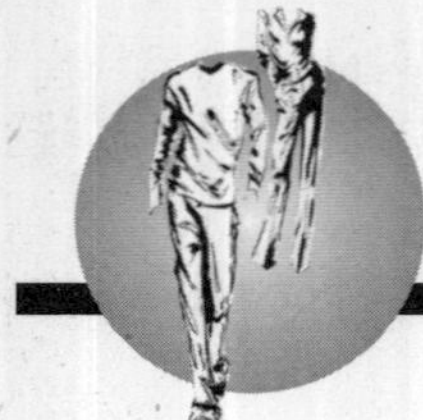

Rating Your Shopping Skills

Directions: Are you a smart shopper? Rate your shopping skills by indicating how often you follow each of the guidelines listed below. Mark each item, using the following code. Then check your rating at the bottom.

Always	Often	Sometimes	Never
A	O	S	N

_____ 1. I plan carefully before I buy clothing.

_____ 2. I recognize good quality in clothing when I see it.

_____ 3. I take or wear the clothes I want to match when I shop.

_____ 4. If I buy fads in clothing or accessories, I limit my spending.

_____ 5. I examine the condition of clothes carefully before buying.

_____ 6. I buy clothes that are versatile.

_____ 7. I avoid buying clothes that I rarely wear.

_____ 8. I own a good balance of clothes for casual occasions, school, and dressing up.

_____ 9. I recognize clothes in the colors and styles that flatter me.

_____ 10. Before I try something on, I can tell whether or not it will look good on me.

_____ 11. I am able to fix clothing myself rather than buy something new to replace it.

_____ 12. I read hangtags and labels before I buy.

_____ 13. My clothing purchases show that I am aware of fashion trends.

_____ 14. I know which stores sell the types of clothes I like.

_____ 15. I compare prices when shopping.

_____ 16. I take advantage of clothing sales.

_____ 17. I avoid buying clothes on impulse.

_____ 18. I follow a clothing budget.

Rating: Count the number of "often" and "always" answers you gave, and find your rating below.

Total "Often" and "Always" Answers	Rating
15 to 18	Congratulations! You are a very smart shopper.
11 to 14	You are a good shopper.
7 to 10	Your shopping skills are fair.
6 or less	Your wardrobe could benefit from more careful shopping.

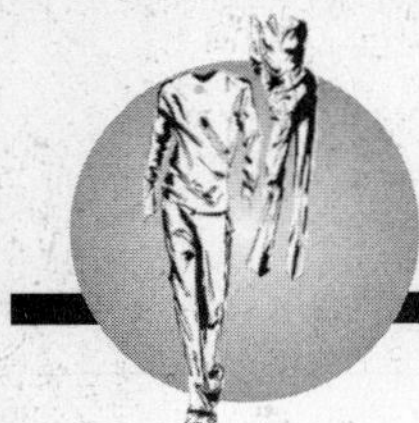

Evaluating Selections

Directions: As you read the chapter, answer the following questions. Later you can use this study guide to review for the Chapter 19 test.

1. Why do people often need a smaller size in more expensive garments? ____________________

____

____

2. On what three factors are sizes for female clothing based? ____________________________

____

3. According to Fig. 19-1, what is the definition of a "petite" woman? ____________________

____

4. On a man's jacket described as having a "relaxed fit," where is the fit "relaxed"? __________

____

5. According to Fig. 19-2, what size category in men's clothing corresponds to women's tall? _______

____

6. What fit factors should you notice when sitting in a garment that you're trying on? __________

____

____

____

7. What is a seam allowance? What is one advantage of a large seam allowance in a garment? _______

____

____

8. What two basic elements indicate quality in a garment? ________________________________

____

9. Why are you advised to crush and pull a corner of a garment you're considering buying? _______

____

(continued on next page)

Chapter 19
Study Guide (continued)

10. What is meant by "workmanship"?____

____

11. Describe stitching that indicates quality in a garment. ___________________________________

____

12. Why is a proper seam finish a sign of good workmanship? _______________________________

____

13. What features will you notice in button closures of a quality garment? ___________________

____

____

____

14. What are two benefits of customized garment fitting with the use of electronic body scanners? _________

____

____

15. How is wrinkle resistance a factor affecting a garment's care needs? _____________________

____

16. Besides quality, what might explain different prices for similar garments? _________________

____

____

17. Give an example of using different resources related to a garment's care needs. ____________

____

____

18. In what way does wearing a garment more often reduce its cost? _________________________

____

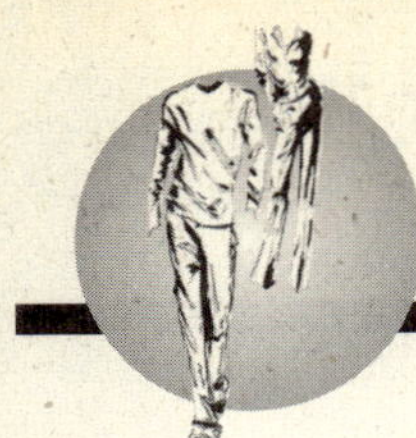

Checking for Quality

Directions: Choose a garment in a clothing store. Rate its quality on each point below by placing a check mark in the appropriate column. Then answer the question that follows.

Questions	Very Good	Good	Fair	Poor	Doesn't Apply
Fabric					
Color even throughout?					
Design printed correctly?					
No snags, pulls, or pills?					
Resists wrinkling?					
Returns to original shape after stretching?					
Cut on grain?					
Suitable for the garment?					
Workmanship					
Stitching even and secure?					
Thread color matches the fabric?					
Fabric design matches throughout the garment?					
Seams smooth and flat?					
Seam allowances at least 1/2-inch (1.3-cm) wide or finished with overlock seam?					
Seams finished to prevent fraying?					
Darts smooth, flat, and point toward fullest part of the body?					
Facings smooth, flat, and invisible from the outside?					
Collar well made?					
Fasteners securely sewn and easy to operate?					
Trims sewn on securely?					
Hem straight and even?					
Hem invisible from the outside?					
Hem allowance finished to prevent raveling?					
Garment free of spots, stains, rips, and other imperfections?					

Based on your ratings, do you think this garment is a good value? Explain your answer.

____

____

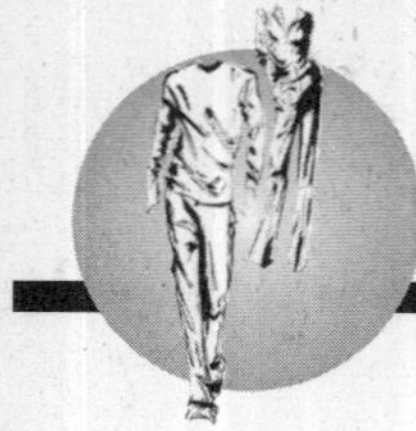

Cost Per Wearing

Directions: Estimating the cost per wearing can be helpful when buying clothes. Read the following situations and answer the questions that follow.

Situation 1—Choosing a Dress. A teen is shopping for a dress that she estimates she will wear about 12 times per year. She has narrowed her choices to two. The *fuchsia dress* costs $68 and would probably need dry cleaning four times a year at about $9 per cleaning. The *turquoise dress* costs $75. It can be machine-washed for about 30¢ per washing and would probably need washing about six times during a year.

________ 1. What is the yearly cost of care for the fuchsia dress?

________ 2. What is the total cost to buy and to care for the fuchsia dress for a year?

________ 3. What is the cost per wearing of the fuchsia dress?

________ 4. What is the yearly cost of care for the turquoise dress?

________ 5. What is the total cost to buy and care for the turquoise dress for a year?

________ 6. What is the cost per wearing of the turquoise dress?

Situation 2—Choosing a Sweater. A teen is deciding which of two sweaters to buy. He will wear it about once a week for five months of the year (20 wearings). The *green-and-navy argyle sweater* costs $33. Dry cleaning would cost $5.50, and the sweater would need about three cleanings each season. The *light blue sweater* costs $39 and can be hand-washed, which would need to be done about six times at a cost of 10¢ for each washing.

7. Calculate the cost per wearing of each sweater in the space below. Circle your answers.

Green-and-Navy Argyle Sweater	Light Blue Sweater

8. In each situation, what is the impact of the cleaning costs? ______________________________

____

9. Do higher cleaning costs necessarily mean a garment is not a good buy? Explain. ______________

____

____

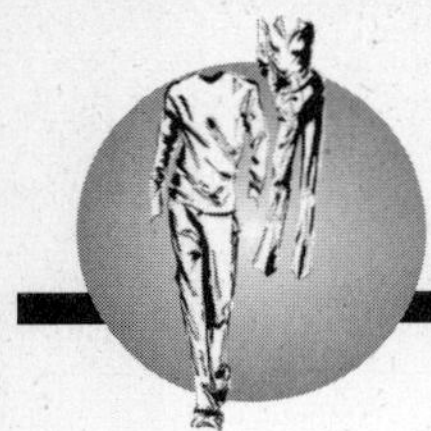

Consumer Responsibilities

Directions: As you read the chapter, answer the following questions. Later you can use this study guide to review for the Chapter 20 test.

1. In what ways does the carelessness of some consumers limit other consumers' right to choose? ___________

____

____

2. What mental habit can help you treat others with consideration? ___________________________________

____

3. How can you help keep clothes clean while trying them on? ______________________________________

____

____

4. How do you show responsibility as a consumer by avoiding unnecessary returns? ___________________

____

____

5. What methods of payment are considered cash transactions? _____________________________________

____

6. What are some disadvantages of paying by check? ____

____

7. What is a debit card? For what are you responsible if your card is lost or stolen? ___________________

____

____

8. Why is paying by money order more costly than paying by check? _________________________________

____

(continued on next page)

Chapter 20
Study Guide (continued)

9. Why are extra costs involved in using credit? _______________________________________

____

10. How is a finance charge figured?____

____

11. Using Fig. 20-7, identify three potential added costs of using credit. ___________________

____

12. How is a consumer's right to choose protected by law? _______________________________

____

13. What is the purpose of the Consumer Product Safety Commission (CSPC)? _____________

____

____

14. What services does the Better Business Bureau provide consumers? ___________________

____

____

____

15. List in order the people or departments you should go to when you have a consumer complaint. ________

____

____

____

16. Identify two laws that directly concern the safety of consumer goods. __________________

____

____

17. How is modern communication technology both an advantage and a challenge for consumers?__________

____

____

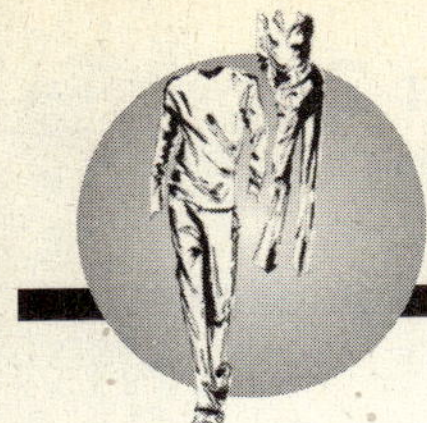

Writing a Complaint Letter

Directions: If you were dissatisfied with a product, would you know how to write a complaint letter? An effective complaint letter contains certain information. Read the guidelines below. Then select one of the situations described at the bottom of the page and write or keyboard a letter of complaint on a separate sheet of paper. Add any details that are missing from the situation. Attach your letter to this activity sheet.

Complaint Letter Checklist	Sample Letter Format
Check off each item as you include it in your letter. ☐ Your name and address. ☐ Name, job title, and location of person to whom you are sending the letter. ☐ Clear explanation of the problem, including how the product or service is defective. ☐ Specific information, such as purchase date, style number, catalog number, or order number. ☐ Steps you have taken to solve the problem. ☐ What you would like done about the problem.	Date Name of addressee Job title Company name Company address *Dear* ______: Body of letter *Sincerely,* Your name Your address

Problem 1: Steaming Mad

Problem: Steam iron (Steam and Dry Model #SS15) fails to produce steam.

Previous action: You returned the iron to the store, Albert's Appliance, and talked to the manager. She said she would return the iron to the manufacturer for repair. That was two months ago. You've heard nothing since.

Problem 2: Fading Hopes?

Problem: The two yards of linen fabric you bought are faded along the lengthwise fold.

Previous action: You spoke to the clerk at Super Sew Store. She said the fabric was sold "as is" and refused to do anything about it.

Problem 3: In the Pink

Problem: The first time you washed a new red shirt, other items in the load were tinged pink. The care label did not say the sweater had to be washed separately.

Previous action: You tried to return the shirt to Cool Cuts clothing store. The clerk would only exchange it for another shirt made by the same company. All the shirts come in very bright colors, which you are afraid may run, too.

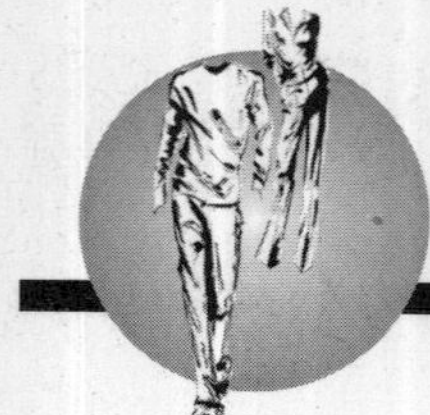

Consumer Protection Laws

Part I. Directions: Listed below are consumer protection laws discussed in the chapter. The statements that follow describe situations related to consumer protection. Match each statement with the most closely related law by placing the correct letter in the blank provided to the left of each number.

A. Textile Fiber Products Identification Act	**E.** Flammable Fabrics Act
B. Care Labeling Rule	**F.** Federal Hazardous Substance Act
C. Wool Products Labeling Act	**G.** Consumer Credit Protection Act
D. Fur Products Labeling Act	**H.** Fair Credit Billing Act

_____ 1. Kitchen curtains are recalled when tests show they don't adequately resist catching fire.

_____ 2. A label sticking out from the back of a baseball cap reads, "Made with pride in the U.S.A."

_____ 3. When a stolen credit card is used, the card owner pays only $50 of the amount charged on the account.

_____ 4. A label sewn into a shirt warns, "Do not iron with steam."

_____ 5. A hangtag on a coat says, "Finest rabbit trim imported from France."

_____ 6. When customers buy a serger on the store's credit plan, a sales associate has them read and sign a paper that identifies the amount of each monthly payment, the finance charge, and the added fees for late payments.

_____ 7. Fabric paints are formulated to avoid using lead.

_____ 8. A label sewn into the side seam of a jacket reads, "Dry clean only."

_____ 9. After a consumer notifies her credit card company that she was charged twice for one pair of slacks, her account is credited with the purchase price.

_____ 10. A label on a winter scarf reads, "50% pure wool, 50% recycled wool."

_____ 11. Responding to consumer demand, a clothing maker replaces decorative buttons on its children's clothing with colorful stitching.

_____ 12. A shipment of socks is returned to the manufacturer because the label identifies them as being 70% cotton, when they are 60% cotton.

_____ 13. A candle falls onto carpet, smolders, and then goes out without starting a fire.

_____ 14. A consumer decides to hand-wash a shirt because of information on the label.

Part II. Directions: Select a product—either for self or home—that you might like to purchase in the future. Identify at least two consumer protection laws may influence your purchase of this product. Use Internet or print resources to further investigate these laws. What information does your research offer that may help you make a better purchase? Write a brief summary of your investigation on a separate sheet of paper. Attach your paper to this activity sheet.

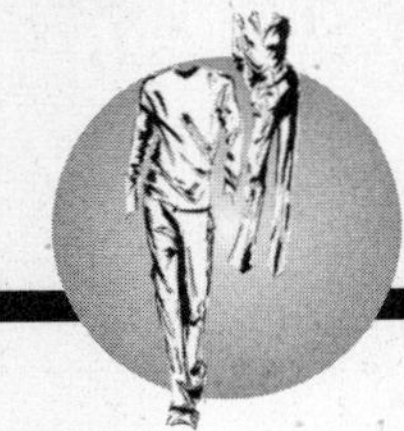

Selecting Clothes for Others

Directions: As you read the chapter, answer the following questions. Later you can use this study guide to review for the Chapter 21 test.

1. Why can buying for others be a challenge? _____________________________________

   ____

2. How can index cards help make gift giving easier? ______________________________

   ____

   ____

3. How is it helpful to notice a person's current wardrobe when giving a gift? _________

   ____

   ____

4. What problems can be solved by asking for a gift receipt? _______________________

   ____

5. What is one advantage of giving accessories as gifts? ___________________________

   ____

6. Why might it be a good idea to buy a seventeen-month-old child a garment that's marked 24 months?

   ____

7. List at least three features that can make a garment unsafe for a young child? _______

   ____

   ____

8. Describe design features that make a garment comfortable for a child to wear. _______

   ____

   ____

(continued on next page)

Clothing: Fashion, Fabrics & Construction Student Activity Manual
Copyright © by The McGraw-Hill Companies, Inc. All rights reserved.

Chapter 21
Study Guide (continued)

9. What features allow clothes to "grow" with a child? Why are they valuable? ______________________

____

____

10. What colors and textures are good choices in children's clothing? ______________________

____

____

11. Why is nonrestrictive clothing important during pregnancy? ______________________

____

____

12. How does the time of year factor into a person's choices when buying maternity fashions? ____________

____

____

13. What different financial situations do older adults have that can affect your choices in clothing gifts for them?

____

____

____

14. How do the physical effects of aging change the clothing needs of some older adults? ____________

____

____

____

15. Why are lightweight fabrics often a good choice for people who use a wheelchair? ____________

____

____

16. List features in a shirt that would help someone with limited energy manage independently. ____________

____

____

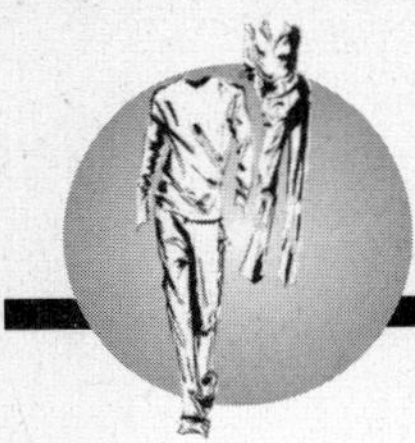

Personal Shopper

Directions: Some clothing stores offer a special service for people who do not have time to shop for additions to their wardrobe. For a fee, a personal shopper picks out clothing and accessories for the customer, or *client*. How do personal shoppers know what clothes their clients want? They first learn about a person's needs, wants, preferences, and activities. Test your skills as a personal shopper. Work with a classmate as your "client." Interview him or her, using the questionnaire below. Then "shop" for at least three new outfits for your client by collecting pictures from magazines, catalogs, or the Internet. Present your client with a poster or notebook of your selections and discuss the results. Then complete the evaluation on the next page.

Client Questionnaire

Name of client: ____

Clothing items desired (rank in order of importance):

Needs	**Wants**
1. ______________________________	1. ______________________________
2. ______________________________	2. ______________________________
3. ______________________________	3. ______________________________
4. ______________________________	4. ______________________________
5. ______________________________	5. ______________________________

Favorite colors: ____

Colors in present wardrobe: ______________________________________

Personality:____

____

____

Activities and hobbies: ____

____

____

Special requests:____

____

____

(continued on next page)

Chapter 21
Activity (continued)

Evaluation

1. What were the main considerations you used in making your selections?_______________

____

____

____

2. Describe two selections presented to your client and explain why you chose them. _______________

____

____

____

____

3. How did your client react to your selections? _______________

____

____

____

4. If you were to work with the same client again, what would you do differently? _______________

____

____

____

5. How would you rate your success as a personal shopper? Explain. _______________

____

____

____

6. Would you like to be a personal shopper for various clients? Why or why not?

____

____

Clothing: Fashion, Fabrics & Construction Student Activity Manual

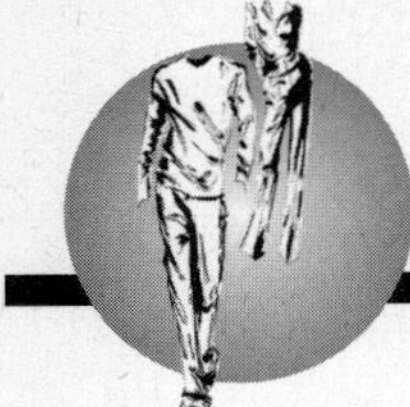

Choosing Clothes for Others

Directions: Deciding what clothing or accessories to buy for others can be a dilemma. Test your ability to select clothing by reading the following situations and answering the questions.

1. A close friend's birthday is coming up, and you want to choose a gift for him. He says he needs clothes. You know that he enjoys the outdoors, and his hobbies are bicycling, reading, and drawing. He also talks about becoming a chef someday. He is adventurous and enjoys new experiences. What are three clothing or accessory gift ideas you have for his birthday? Explain your reasons for choosing each one.

____

____

____

____

____

2. A close family friend has a little boy who will soon be turning three. He is learning to dress himself. You want to give him some new clothes for his birthday. Describe in detail a garment that you would select for him and explain why you made this choice.

____

____

____

____

3. A relative, who is three months pregnant, has limited money to spend on maternity clothing. Her baby is due July 15, and she lives in an area that has cold winters and hot summers. You and other family members want to buy her some maternity clothes for her birthday next week. What types of clothing would be best considering where your relative lives? Include specific examples.

____

____

____

____

(continued on next page)

Clothing: Fashion, Fabrics & Construction Student Activity Manual
Copyright © by The McGraw-Hill Companies, Inc. All rights reserved.

Chapter 21
Activity (continued)

4. You often buy birthday and holiday gifts for family and friends, but the cost is becoming a problem. Suggest five clothing or accessory gifts you could give that would keep costs to a minimum. Ideas could be related to clothing or handmade items.

____

____

____

5. A neighbor of yours recently retired and now lives on a fixed income. She is like a mother to you, and you want to get her a small gift for Mother's Day. You would like to get something practical that she can use—a simple garment or accessory. What will you do?

____

____

____

____

6. A friend broke his leg and is wearing a cast. What alterations could you make in his clothing to make dressing easier?

____

____

____

7. After hip surgery, an elderly family member is using a wheelchair. Your family has decided to lift her spirits with a new outfit. What would the outfit you buy be like?

____

____

____

8. A friend of your family, who is visually impaired, is in his twenties. He is moving into an apartment, where he will live alone for the first time. Family members are buying him some new clothes for his birthday. How could they customize their gifts to help this young man?

____

____

____

Clothing: Fashion, Fabrics & Construction Student Activity Manual
Copyright © by The McGraw-Hill Companies, Inc. All rights reserved.

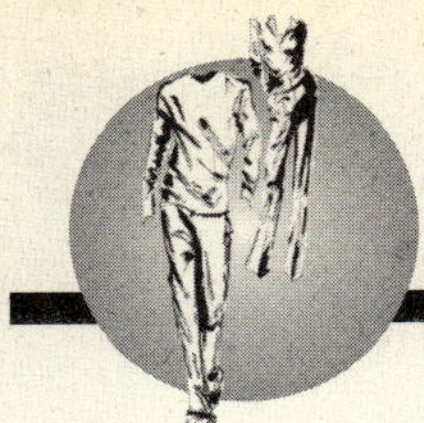

Is Fashion Merchandising for You?

Part I. Directions: Read the feature on careers in fashion merchandising on pages 372–375 in your textbook. The checklist below lists several qualities that a person desiring to work in the field of fashion merchandising should possess. To find out whether you might be a good fit for this career field, place a check mark in the appropriate column for each quality.

Quality	Definitely	Mostly	Somewhat	Not at all
1. I am very interested in fashion.				
2. I tend to lead rather than follow.				
3. I can "roll with the punches."				
4. I enjoy learning different skills.				
5. I am interested in working with others.				
6. I see new technology as an asset				

Part II. Directions: Below are some skills a person desiring to work in the field of fashion merchandising should possess. Evaluate your own skills by giving one example of how you demonstrate each skill.

7. Interpersonal communication: ____

____

8. Organization: ____

9. Management: ____

10. Decision making and problem solving: ____

11. Mathematical ability: ____

12. Analytical thinking: ____

13. Mental and physical stamina: ____

14. Based on this self-evaluation of your qualities and skills, do you have what it takes to make a career in fashion merchandising? What qualities and skills would you need to develop that you do not yet possess? Do you think this field would interest you? Why or why not? Write your answers in the space provided. If necessary, use an additional sheet of paper and attach it to this activity.

____

____

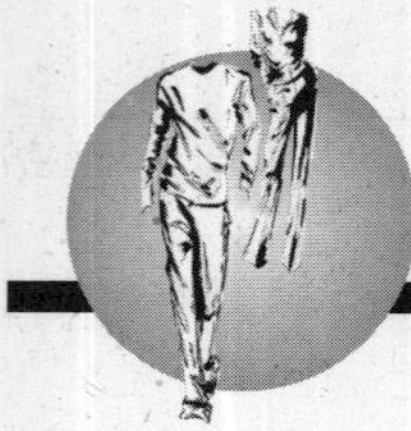

Writing a Letter of Inquiry

Part I. Directions: Imagine that you are looking for a position in fashion merchandising. During your research of companies you come across some companies that you think you might be interested in working for, but they are not advertising any openings right now. You decide to write a letter of inquiry to these companies to establish some contacts and find out if they expect to have any openings. The guidelines below explain what a letter of inquiry is and how to construct one.

What Is a Letter of Inquiry?

- An individualized, personal letter sent to a specific employer to find out about possible job openings that are not advertised
- An opportunity to show a potential employer how you can benefit the company
- A chance to get your foot in the door without a lot of competition, as you are looking for unadvertised openings
- An opportunity to build contacts in your career field

What Is It Not?

- A vague inquiry about any job openings
- A repetition of what is on your resume
- A generic letter that could be mass-sent to several companies

What Does a Letter of Inquiry Include?

- A salutation addressed to a specific person
- A first paragraph that explains the reason you are writing and indicates the source who referred you, if applicable
- A second paragraph that offers a brief explanation of your accomplishments and skills, relevant to the position you are inquiring about
- A third paragraph that indicates that you have researched the company and have something specific to offer it
- A strong, positive closing that indicates that you will call within a specified time period to arrange a meeting to talk about the company's potential needs and how you can meet them

Other Things to Remember

- Address the letter to a particular person if possible. Make sure the person's name is spelled correctly and you use his or her title. Do not address to "Dear Sir or Madam."
- Use simple, direct language and traditional business letter format.
- Use language that shows your enthusiasm and motivation.
- Keep it to one page or less.
- Double-check spelling, grammar, and punctuation.
- Include a copy of your resume.
- Call when you said you would call. Refer to your letter in your phone call.

Part II. Directions: After reading the above guidelines, use word-processing software to keyboard a letter of inquiry to a company of your choosing. Print a copy of your letter and attach it to this activity sheet.

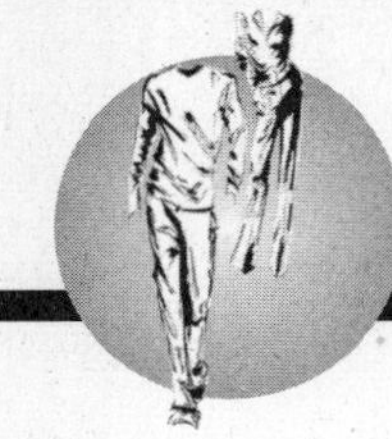

Career Preparation

Directions: As you read the chapter, answer the following questions. Later you can use this study guide to review for the Chapter 22 test.

1. Why is discovering your aptitudes valuable for choosing a career? ________________________________

____

2. How can interest surveys help you choose a career? ____

____

3. Why is a future fashion designer wise to work hard in all school subjects? ________________________

____

____

4. What important information can you learn by mapping out a career path? _________________________

____

____

____

5. What facts do you need to evaluate and compare training programs? _____________________________

____

____

6. What do shadowing and part-time jobs have in common? ______________________________________

____

____

7. What are some good sources of ads for job openings? ____

____

8. Why might you contact an employer that is not advertising job openings? _________________________

____

(continued on next page)

Chapter 22
Study Guide (continued)

9. What information may an employer legally require on a job application form? What facts cannot be required?

____

____

10. Name two career research Web sites sponsored by the U.S. Department of Labor. ___________

____

____

11. What information should you have on hand to fill out a job application form? ________________

____

____

12. Why is the skills format a popular way to organize résumés?___________________________

____

____

13. Besides past jobs, what kind of activities might you list on a résumé? ____________________

____

____

14. What information should be included in a cover letter?________________________________

____

____

15. How can researching a business help you make a good impression at an interview?____________

____

16. How should you follow up after an interview? _____________________________________

____

17. Describe an outfit that's suitable for an interview. ___________________________________

____

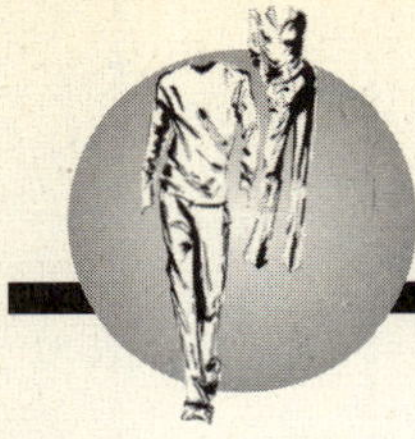

Career Interviews

Directions: Select three people to interview about their careers. Include two people with at least ten years of work experience. Use the questions on the next page to write responses for one interview. For the other interviews, write responses on separate paper and attach them to this activity. After completing the interviews, answer the questions below.

1. Do you think changing careers is common in the work world? Explain. ______________________________

____

____

2. What impact do training and education have on careers? ____________________________________

____

____

3. What role does technology play in careers today? ____

____

____

4. What do you think contributes to a satisfying career? _____________________________________

____

____

5. What did you learn from the interviews that will be helpful to you? _________________________

____

____

(continued on next page)

Name____ Date________________ Class _______________

Interview Questions

Person interviewed _______________________________ **Total years of work experience** _______________

1. Please describe your current career for me. ____

____

____

2. What other work experiences have you had? What caused any career changes? _______________

____

____

3. What education and training are needed for your work? _________________________________

____

____

4. What skills are needed in your work? ____

____

____

5. How does technology impact your work? What changes in technology have you seen? _____________

____

____

____

6. Has your career given you a sense of accomplishment and satisfaction? Please explain. _____________

____

____

____

7. What advice would you give to someone who is planning a career? _________________________

____

____

____

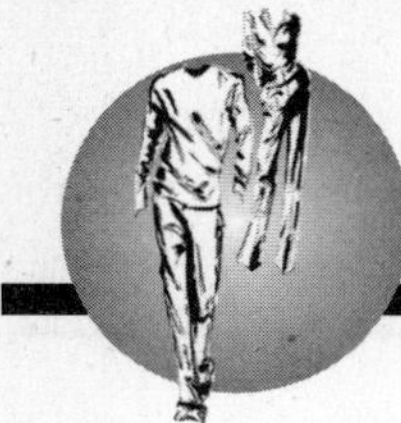

Job Application

Directions: Complete the job application below. Keep the following points in mind:
- To avoid mistakes, read the entire application before you begin.
- Spell correctly, using a dictionary if necessary.
- Always use ink rather than pencil.
- Printing or typing is usually preferred over handwriting.
- Be prepared to give the names, addresses, and telephone numbers of references.

Application for Employment

Date: ____________

PERSONAL DATA:

LAST	FIRST	MIDDLE	Home Phone: ______________
Name:____			Business Phone: ___________

NUMBER	STREET	CITY	STATE	ZIP

Permanent Address: ____

Social Security Number: ______________________ If under 18 years of age state your age: ________

If not a U.S. citizen, do you have a visa permitting you to work? ____________ Yes ☐ No ☐ Number:________

WORK INTERESTS:

Position Desired:________________________ Willing to Relocate? Yes ☐ No ☐

Referred By: ___________________________ Willing to Travel? Yes ☐ No ☐

Salary Desired: ____________ Keyboarding Speed:(wpm) ________ Other Business Skills: ______________

Have you previously applied to or worked for ______________ or an affiliated Company? Yes ☐ No ☐

Company and Location: ________________________ Dates: ______________

EDUCATION:

	NAME & ADDRESS OF SCHOOL	MAJOR COURSE	LAST GRADE COMPLETED	GRADUATED/ DEGREE	STILL ATTENDING
HIGH SCHOOL					
COLLEGE					
OTHER					

(continued on next page)

Chapter 22
Activity (continued)

<table>
<tr><td colspan="3" align="center">U.S. MILITARY SERVICE:</td></tr>
<tr><td colspan="3">Have you ever served in the Armed Forces?   Yes ☐   No ☐   If Yes: Active Duty From___________   To __________</td></tr>
<tr><td colspan="3" align="center">EMPLOYMENT HISTORY:</td></tr>
<tr><td colspan="3">LIST BELOW YOUR FORMER EMPLOYERS. BEGIN WITH THE PRESENT EMPLOYER.
NOTE ANY PERIODS OF UNEMPLOYMENT.</td></tr>
<tr><td>1. EMPLOYER:</td><td>DATE EMPLOYED</td><td>POSITION:</td></tr>
<tr><td>ADDRESS:</td><td>FROM: TO:</td><td>MAJOR JOB DUTIES:</td></tr>
<tr><td>SUPERVISOR:</td><td></td><td></td></tr>
<tr><td>MAY WE CONTACT?</td><td>SALARY</td><td></td></tr>
<tr><td>REASON FOR LEAVING:</td><td>$ TO $</td><td></td></tr>
<tr><td>2. EMPLOYER:</td><td>DATE EMPLOYED</td><td>POSITION:</td></tr>
<tr><td>ADDRESS:</td><td>FROM: TO:</td><td>MAJOR JOB DUTIES:</td></tr>
<tr><td>SUPERVISOR:</td><td></td><td></td></tr>
<tr><td>MAY WE CONTACT?</td><td>SALARY</td><td></td></tr>
<tr><td>REASON FOR LEAVING:</td><td>$ TO $</td><td></td></tr>
<tr><td>3. EMPLOYER:</td><td>DATE EMPLOYED</td><td>POSITION:</td></tr>
<tr><td>ADDRESS:</td><td>FROM: TO:</td><td>MAJOR JOB DUTIES:</td></tr>
<tr><td>SUPERVISOR:</td><td></td><td></td></tr>
<tr><td>MAY WE CONTACT?</td><td>SALARY</td><td></td></tr>
<tr><td>REASON FOR LEAVING:</td><td>$ TO $</td><td></td></tr>
<tr><td colspan="3">Have you ever been convicted of a crime, offense, or violation, other than parking violations, within the last five years that was not sealed or annulled by a court?   Yes ☐   No ☐
If yes, list all convictions, showing date, court, and name of offense. Conviction of a crime is not necessarily a bar to employment.

____</td></tr>
<tr><td colspan="3">I agree that the company may, as part of the verification of this application, contact the educational institutions and references above. I understand that falsification of any part of this application is justifiable grounds for immediate dismissal. If employed, I understand that the first ninety days (90) of my employment constitute a probationary period and, if employed, I understand that I am employed at the will of management, and management retains the right to alter the terms and conditions of my employment at any time.

Date: _____________________   Signature: ________________________________</td></tr>
</table>

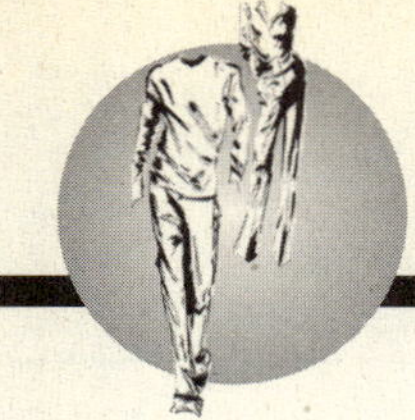

Answering Interview Questions

Directions: Interviewing for a job is easier if you have practiced answers to questions that may be asked. Choose one of the jobs below or pick a different one. Assume you have applied for the job, you are qualified, and you have been called for an interview. Identify the job and create a description of what the company is like. Then write answers to the questions below as though you are in an actual interview. Use complete sentences. Imagine any details that are needed to answer the questions. Afterwards, compare responses with class members and share ideas for handling difficult questions.

Sales associate in a large department store	Sewing machine operator	Textile chemist
Graphic designer	Inspector	Stock clerk
Fashion copywriter	Fashion designer	FCS teacher

What job are you applying for? ____

Describe the business/company. ____

____

Interview Questions

1. Tell me a little about yourself. ____

____

____

2. What do you know about our company? ______________________________________

____

____

3. Why do you want to work here? ____

____

____

4. What did you like least about your last job? _________________________________

____

____

(continued on next page)

5. What did you think of your last supervisor? ____

____

6. What is a weakness of yours? ____

____

____

7. How do you handle conflict? ____

____

____

8. What do you think makes a good team member? ______________________________________

____

____

9. Describe how you handled a challenging work situation. ________________________________

____

____

10. What are your short- and long-term goals? ____

____

____

11. Why should I hire you for this position? ____

____

____

12. What would you like to gain from working for our company? ____________________________

____

____

13. How do I rate as an interviewer?____

____

____

          Clothing: Fashion, Fabrics & Construction Student Activity Manual

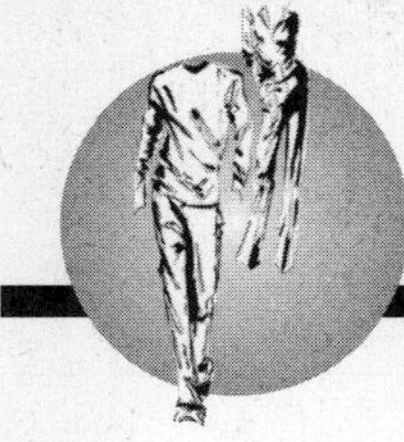

Success on the Job

Directions: As you read the chapter, answer the following questions. Later you can use this study guide to review for the Chapter 23 test.

1. List some technological skills that are valued by employers. _______________________________________

____

____

2. What actions show a worker is reliable? ____

____

____

____

3. How do you show others respect on the job? ____

____

____

____

4. How is flexibility related to workplace success? ____

____

____

____

5. What should workers think about before showing initiative?______________________________________

____

____

6. Give examples of ways that employees use leadership skills. ______________________________________

____

____

(continued on next page)

Chapter 23
Study Guide *(continued)*

7. Name two organizations that help students develop leadership skills. _______________________

____

____

8. Why would copying company software for personal use be considered unethical? ____________

____

9. What do employers offer to help workers develop skills? _______________________________

____

____

10. Why is it important to understand the relationship between work and personal life? __________

____

____

____

11. How does procrastination hinder efforts to balance work and personal life?_________________

____

____

12. How is dovetailing activities helpful for balancing conflicting demands? ___________________

____

____

13. Why is having realistic expectations important for managing obligations? __________________

____

____

____

14. Give two examples of how a support system can help with personal management. ____________

____

____

____

   Clothing: Fashion, Fabrics & Construction Student Activity Manual

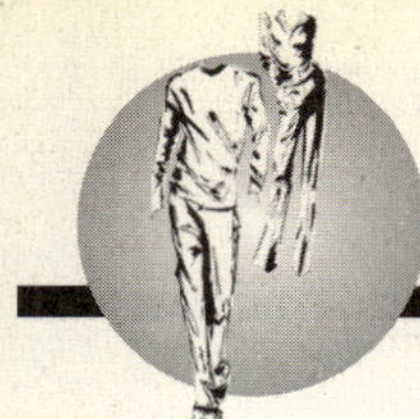

Qualities for Success

Directions: Reliability, flexibility, teamwork, and initiative are a few qualities of valued employees. Remember these and other helpful traits as you read the situations below. Describe a constructive response for each teen employee and explain how it demonstrates a positive quality.

1. **Teen A** is a stock clerk at a sporting goods store. He just spent the morning inspecting, counting, recording, and tagging a new shipment of jogging suits. He is looking forward to quitting time when his supervisor announces that the shipment they expected two days ago just arrived. It needs to be readied for the sales floor as soon as possible.

   Response: ____

   Quality: ____

   ____

2. **Teen B** is taking a fourth bottle of perfume from the display case to show a customer. Nearby, a coworker has been ringing up sales for the last twenty minutes, and more customers are waiting. Both work for salary plus commission. Making sales is important for income and promotion. Finally the customer says, "These are so expensive. Can you show me something for less?"

   Response: ____

   Quality: ____

   ____

3. **Teen C** is a sales associate at a family shoe store. He has noticed parents struggling with children who get bored and irritable. He has also had to stop children from getting into shoe displays. The store manager tells him that other workers, as well as customers, have complained about the same problem.

   Response: ____

   Quality: ____

   ____

4. After high school graduation, **Teen D** became a trainee in the human resources office of a store where she had worked as a sales associate. She now has access to employees' personal records. Two of her former coworkers have complained about a third worker, who is a good employee but rather annoying. They have hinted that the teen should look for something in his personal files that could be used to get him transferred or pressure him to quit.

   Response: ____

   ____

   Quality: ____

Retail Math Skills

Directions: Many careers in fashion start with a position as a sales associate or something similar. Many such positions require math skills like those in the situations below. Practice your retail math skills as you read each situation and answer the questions that follow.

> **Situation 1.** You work for a dry cleaner. A customer brings in items and asks what it would cost to have them all cleaned. The prices are as follows: *slacks*, $6.75; *coat*, $12.50; and *2 sweaters*, $6.25 each. There is also a 8% sales tax.

_________________________ 1. What will the customer's total bill be?

> **Situation 2.** You work as a sales associate in a department store. A customer returns a sweater, priced at $29.95. To replace it, she has chosen a skirt and blouse. The blouse costs $24.95, and the skirt is on sale for $18.50. A 6% sales tax applies to all items.

_________________________ 2. What is the total cost of the sweater?

_________________________ 3. What is the total cost of the blouse and skirt?

_________________________ 4. Does the customer receive a refund or owe on the exchange?

_________________________ 5. How much is the refund or the amount she owes?

> **Situation 3.** You are a fabric store employee. A customer brings the items below to the checkout counter and asks whether $25 will pay for everything. Calculate the cost of each and the total cost of all the items. The prices already include tax.

_________________________ 6. 1¾ yards of a cotton print at $4.49 per yard.

_________________________ 7. 2¼ yards of a denim fabric at $7.50 per yard.

_________________________ 8. Four packages of buttons at 99¢ per package.

_________________________ 9. Two yards of trim at $1.24 per yard.

_________________________ 10. Two zippers at $1.79 each.

_________________________ 11. Will $25 cover the entire purchase? If so, how much change is the customer owed? If not, how much more must the customer pay?

_________________________ 12. In the store flyer, the customer finds a coupon good for 15% off the entire amount. Using this coupon and the $25, does the customer owe money or receive money back? What amount?

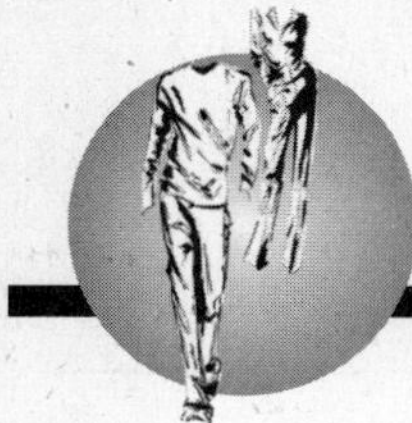

Fashion Entrepreneurs

Directions: As you read the chapter, answer the following questions. Later you can use this study guide to review for the Chapter 24 test.

1. How are achievement and motivation related in the successful entrepreneur? ___________________
____

2. List at least four tasks that require an entrepreneur to have organizational and management skills.
____
____

3. What personal traits help entrepreneurs face the risk involved in running a business?______________
____
____

4. Why do entrepreneurs need good communication skills? ____
____
____

5. List some fashion-related services that are often provided by entrepreneurs. ______________________
____
____

6. Why is location so important to a business's success?____
____
____

7. What advantages does a mail-order business offer the entrepreneur who works on a small budget?
____
____

8. How does market research help identify a target audience? _____________________________________
____

(continued on next page)

Chapter 24
Study Guide (continued)

9. How is the Small Business Administration a resource for entrepreneurs? _________________________

____

____

10. What information does an entrepreneur need to give a potential lender? _________________________

____

____

____

11. Where can entrepreneurs learn about business regulations? _________________________________

____

____

12. Why might zoning laws be a special concern for the owner of an in-home business? ______________

____

13. What costs are included in operating expenses? ____

____

14. How can competitors' prices be used as a gauge when deciding what to charge for an item or service?

____

____

15. Why is record keeping important to business success? ______________________________________

____

____

____

16. What items are included in a good business plan? ____

____

____

____

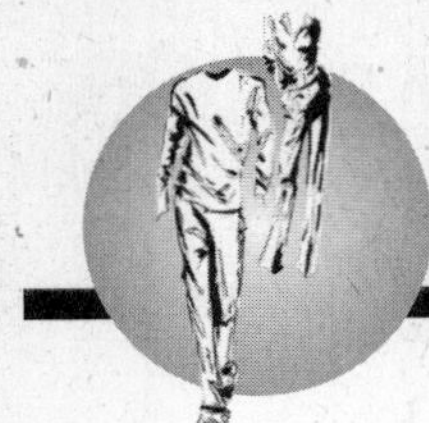

Challenges and Opportunities

Directions: As you've read, entrepreneurs need certain qualities to handle the demands that await them daily. Read each situation described below. Then choose qualities from the chapter that would be particularly useful in each situation. Name the qualities you select and explain how or why each one would be helpful.

1. A friend who owns a clothing shop offers to let you run your sewing and alteration business in a small, little-used room of her store. In exchange, you must give her clients first priority and reduced rates for alterations on items purchased at the store.

____

____

____

2. You have just returned from buying ad space in some local newspapers. The ad, which you designed, announces the opening of your personalized clothing business later this month. You find a call on your answering machine from the company that sells heat-transfer printers. Due to some unknown problem with the manufacturer, the printer you ordered will not be shipped until early next month.

____

____

____

3. You own an online mail-order business specializing in youthful, trendy styles. You have noticed that a few designers are starting to use fringe, silver, and turquoise in their garments. You have not heard or read anything about this look, but you suspect it is growing more popular.

____

____

____

4. You have found just the right location for starting up a small shop where you want to sell handcrafted jewelry, but the place is a disaster. It is in one corner of a large warehouse that is being divided into shops. You have no extra money, and you are new in town.

____

____

____

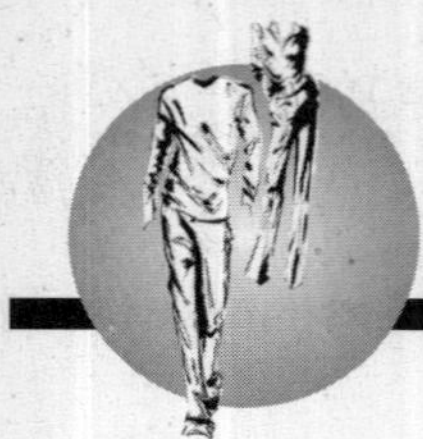

Writing a Press Release

Directions: A successful business begins with planning and preparation, but it takes flight with promotion. One inexpensive and effective means of promotion is a *press release*, an article that describes an event, such as the opening of a business. Think about a business you might start. Then write a press release to send to area newspapers. You will want to tell readers everything they need to know about your business and encourage them to become your customers—in about 250 words or less. Use the following guidelines:

1. Start with a brief, attention-getting introduction.
2. Continue with the most important facts: WHO is starting the business? WHAT is the product or service? WHEN is the business opening? WHERE is the business located?
3. End with details and background information. For example: Why did you decide to start this business? What skills and experience do you have? How can the business benefit your customers and the community?

Press Release

____

____

____

____

____

____

____

____

____

____

____

____

____

____

____

____

Clothing: Fashion, Fabrics & Construction Student Activity Manual

Global Marketplace

Directions: As you read the chapter, answer the following questions. Later you can use this study guide to review for the Chapter 25 test.

1. What is the relationship between imports, exports, and balance of trade?_________________

____

____

2. Why might a United States clothing maker establish a factory in a foreign country? ________

____

____

____

3. Why might a manufacturer contract with smaller companies to produce its goods?_________

____

____

4. Why are undocumented immigrants especially vulnerable to sweatshop labor? ___________

____

____

5. What factors make it possible for sweatshops to continue to operate? _________________

____

____

6. What situation in developing countries makes child-labor laws harder to enforce? _________

____

7. How do counterfeiters hurt companies and consumers? _____________________________

____

____

(continued on next page)

Chapter 25
Study Guide (continued)

8. How do companies protect against counterfeiting? _______________________________

____

____

9. How are tariffs determined? ____

10. Prior to the establishment of the World Trade Organization (WTO), what did it mean to a country to gain

most-favored-nation status? ____

____

____

11. What is the goal of the World Trade Organization (WTO)? _______________________

____

____

12. How does merging help companies stay competitive? _________________________

____

____

13. How does the Occupational Safety and Health Administration help keep workers safe? _______________

____

____

____

14. What is the *Encouraging Environmental Excellence* program? _________________

____

____

____

15. What obstacle do textile product makers face in adopting environmentally friendly practices? __________

____

Clothing: Fashion, Fabrics & Construction Student Activity Manual

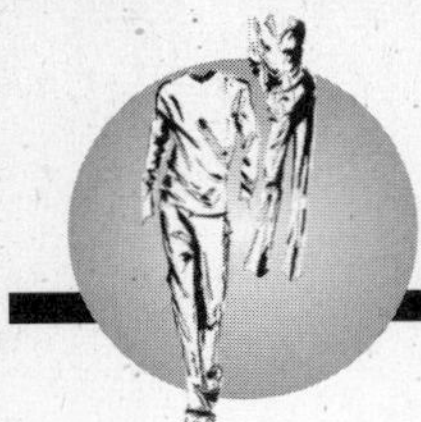

Clothing Origins

Directions: Clothing is made all over the world. A quick "trip" through your closet will show where your clothing originated. Examine the labels on ten garments in your home and list the countries that you find named. You may see more than one country listed if the fabric originated in a separate location. Place a check mark under the continent where each country is located. After your survey is completed, answer the questions on the next page.

Garment	Country	North America	South America	Europe	Asia	Africa	Australia

(continued on next page)

Clothing: Fashion, Fabrics & Construction Student Activity Manual

Analyzing Your Survey

1. Did you find any pattern to where your clothing originated? For example, did less expensive clothing tend to originate from the same country or region of the world? Did clothing for different genders originate in different locations? Explain.

____

____

____

____

____

2. How frequently did you find that the fabric originated in one country, but the garment was assembled in another country? Give examples.

____

____

____

____

3. What is the economic impact on the United States of purchasing clothing produced overseas? What is the impact on countries overseas?

____

____

____

____

4. Compare the results of your survey to those of classmates. How were your findings similar and different?

____

____

____

____

Clothing: Fashion, Fabrics & Construction Student Activity Manual

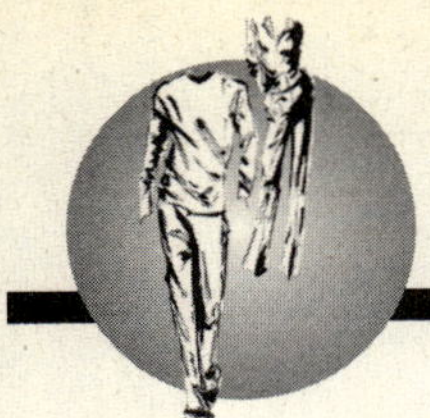

Is Communication and Education for You?

Part I. Directions: Read the feature on careers in communication and education on pages 432–435 in your textbook. The checklist below lists several qualities that a person desiring to work in the field of communication and education should possess. To find out whether you might be a good fit for this career field, place a check mark in the appropriate column for each quality.

Quality	Definitely	Mostly	Somewhat	Not at all
1. I am curious about how and why things happen.				
2. I like a fair amount of independence in my work.				
3. To me, a deadline is a tool for time management.				
4. I enjoy learning as much as teaching and doing				
5. I can use constructive criticism to my benefit.				
6. Seeing the results of my work is more rewarding than money.				

Part II. Directions: Below are some skills a person desiring to work in the field of communication and education should possess. Evaluate your own skills by giving one example of how you demonstrate each skill.

7. Communication: ____

8. Management: ____

9. Organization: ____

10. Creativity: ____

11. Flexibility: ____

12. Self-discipline: ____

13. Self-confidence: ____

14. Based on this self-evaluation of your qualities and skills, do you have what it takes to make a career in communication and education? What qualities and skills would you need to develop that you do not yet possess? Do you think this field would interest you? Why or why not? Write your answers on a separate sheet of paper and attach it to this activity.

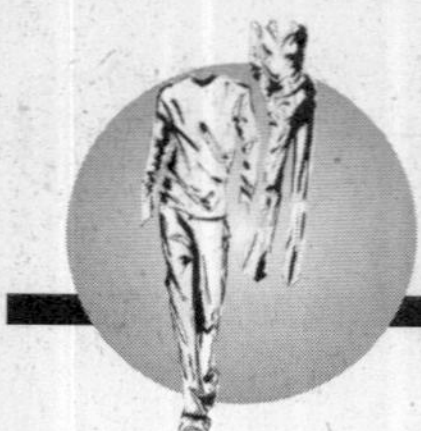

Jobs in Communication and Education

Unit 7
Activity

Part I. Directions: Look for job listings in fashion communication and education via the Internet (see the tips on page 383 of your textbook). Find eight to ten listings, study the ads, and answer the questions below. **Choose two of the ads to answer the following questions.**

1. **Job Position A:** ____

2. What kind of education and/or training is required? ___________________________

3. Is this an entry-level position, or is experience required? What type of experience is specified?

____

4. What requirements listed in the ad are similar to the qualities and skills listed for this field in Activity 1?

____

5. List two responsibilities of this position.___________________________________

____

6. **Job Position B:** ____

7. What kind of education and/or training is required? ___________________________

8. Is this an entry-level position, or is experience required? What type of experience is specified?

____

9. What requirements listed in the ad are similar to the qualities and skills listed for this field in Activity 1?

____

10. List two responsibilities of this position.___________________________________

____

Part II. Directions: Answer the following general questions about all the ads you located. Write your answers on a separate sheet of paper and attach it to this activity.

11. In addition to the two ads discussed above, what other job openings did you find?

12. In general, what level of education/training and experience did most of the jobs require?

13. Describe the pay ranges if mentioned in the listings.

14. Using clues from the ads about work environments (for example, "fast paced," "team player"), make some generalizations about the type of working conditions for positions in this field.

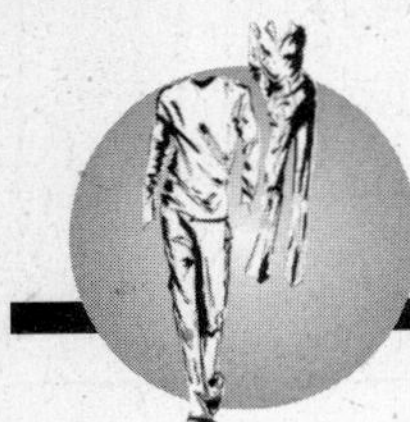

Selecting a Pattern

Directions: As you read the lesson, answer the following questions. Later you can use this study guide to review for the Part 1 Handbook test.

1. What four factors should you consider when picking a pattern? ___________________________

____

____

____

2. Why do most patterns show more than one view? _____________________________________

____

____

3. How do you locate a pattern envelope after choosing it in a catalog? ____________________

____

____

4. How can you decide whether the style of a garment from a certain pattern will look good on you?

____

____

____

____

5. What tool should be used to take body measurements? ________________________________

____

6. What measurements are needed to determine the correct pattern size you need?____________

____

____

(continued on next page)

Lesson 1
Study Guide (continued)

7. What factors determine your figure type? ____

____

8. Should you wear shoes when measuring your height? _________________________________

____

9. Explain how to take a waist measurement. ____

____

____

____

10. How should you choose a pattern if your measurements fall between two sizes shown? ______________

____

____

____

11. On a pattern envelope yardage chart, why might you find several amounts listed? ______________

____

____

____

12. Why are multisized patterns especially useful? _____________________________________

____

____

____

13. What would happen if a pants pattern didn't include wearing ease? _____________________

____

____

Name____

Clothing: Fashion, Fabrics & Construction Student Activity Manual

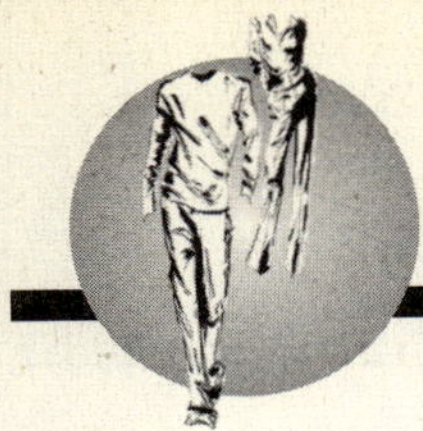

Choosing a Pattern

Directions: The first step in a successful sewing project is selecting an appropriate pattern in the correct size. Start by taking accurate measurements. Remember that measurements are private information that does not have to be shared with others. After recording your measurements in the chart below, visit a pattern company's Web site or look at a pattern catalog for guidance in choosing the correct size. Answer the questions in this activity as you decide which pattern to choose for your project.

Personal Measurements	
Height	
Bust/chest	
Waist	
Hips	
Neck (males)	
Back waist length (females)	
In-seam	
Out-seam	
Sleeve	

Analyzing Patterns

1. Compare your measurements with charts from the pattern industry and determine your size category, or figure type. Examples are misses, juniors, children's, and men's. Write your figure type here.

   ____

2. What size is closest to your measurements? ____

3. What size do you need for pants or a skirt? ____

4. What pattern size will you purchase? If it is not the size you listed in question 2 or 3, explain why.

   ____

   ____

   ____

(continued on next page)

Clothing: Fashion, Fabrics & Construction Student Activity Manual
Copyright © by The McGraw-Hill Companies, Inc. All rights reserved.

Lesson 1
Activity (continued)

5. Browse the pattern catalog or Web sites and find three patterns that appeal to you. List their numbers and describe each one.

____

____

____

____

6. Which of the three patterns is most suitable for your level of sewing skills? Why?

____

____

____

____

7. Which of the three patterns would be most flattering to you? Explain.

____

____

____

____

8. Which of the garments would be the most costly to make? The least costly? Would you be likely to make more than one of the pattern views?

____

____

____

9. Considering your responses to the last three questions, put your pattern choice below.

View ____

Pattern number ____

Pattern company ____

Instructor's approval ____Date ____________

Selecting Fabric

Directions: As you read the lesson, answer the following questions. Later you can use this study guide to review for the Part 1 Handbook test.

1. What is a bolt? ____

____

2. Where can you find information about the types of fabrics that would work well with a pattern?

____

____

3. How do you use a stretch gauge? ____

____

____

____

4. How can you test whether a fabric will work with a pattern that has pleats? ___________

____

____

____

5. What flaws should you check for when looking at a fabric? _______________________

____

____

____

6. How can reading the end of the bolt help you choose a suitable fabric for a pattern? _______

____

____

____

(continued on next page)

Clothing: Fashion, Fabrics & Construction Student Activity Manual
Copyright © by The McGraw-Hill Companies, Inc. All rights reserved.

Lesson 2
Study Guide (continued)

7. Describe the characteristics of fabrics that are good choices for new sewers.________________

____

____

8. Why might a loosely woven fabric prove frustrating for a first-time sewer? ________________

____

____

9. How can you tell that a fabric will suit your appearance and activities? ___________________

____

____

____

____

____

10. Why is it important to note the fabric width needed for a pattern? ___________________

____

____

____

____

11. Why might a velvet garment appear to be made with fabric pieces of slightly different colors?

____

____

____

____

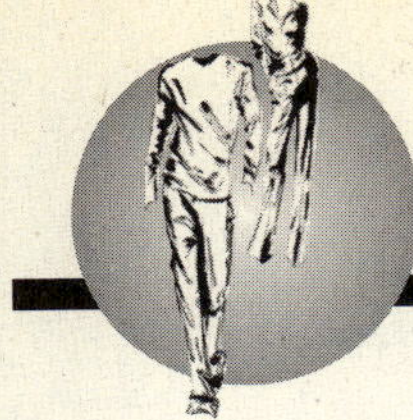

Comparing Fabrics

Directions: For a successful sewing project, selecting an appropriate fabric is just as important as making a wise pattern choice. Find four fabrics that you like and compare their suitability for the pattern you chose in the Lesson 1 activity. Then answer the questions that follow. You may find it helpful to refer to Chapters 11-13 in the text as you complete this activity.

Pattern number_________________ **Pattern company** _________________________________ **View** ___________

Fabric suggestions from pattern envelope ____

____

____

Fabric Number 1

Description _________________________________

____

Price per yard ____________ Sale price? ☐ yes ☐ no

Fabric width __________ Yardage needed _________

Total cost of fabric for garment ________________

Comments_________________________________

____

____

Fabric Number 2

Description _________________________________

____

Price per yard ____________ Sale price? ☐ yes ☐ no

Fabric width __________ Yardage needed _________

Total cost of fabric for garment ________________

Comments_________________________________

____

____

Fabric Number 3

Description _________________________________

____

Price per yard ____________ Sale price? ☐ yes ☐ no

Fabric width __________ Yardage needed _________

Total cost of fabric for garment ________________

Comments_________________________________

____

____

Fabric Number 4

Description _________________________________

____

Price per yard ____________ Sale price? ☐ yes ☐ no

Fabric width __________ Yardage needed _________

Total cost of fabric for garment ________________

Comments_________________________________

____

____

(continued on next page)

Lesson 2
Activity (continued)

1. Describe, in general terms, the weight, texture, or other significant qualities that the fabric suggestions given on the pattern envelope have in common.

____

____

____

2. Does each fabric you have chosen meet the criteria set by the pattern's fabric suggestions? Explain.

____

____

____

3. Considering your current sewing skills, would any of your four fabric options hinder the success of your project? Explain.

____

____

____

4. Based on the fabric costs, do any exceed what you are willing to spend on the garment? Consider the cost per wearing, too.

____

____

____

5. Which fabric would be most flattering to your appearance? Which meets any special needs (easy care for traveling, comfort in warm weather, etc.)?

____

____

____

6. Which fabric will you choose and why? _______________________________________

____

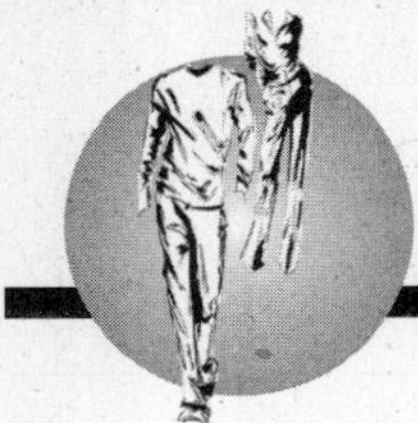

Selecting Notions

Lesson 3
Study Guide

Directions: As you read the lesson, answer the following questions. Later you can use this study guide to review for the Part 1 Handbook test.

1. Describe two factors that help guide your choice of notions. ___________________________

____

____

2. What color thread should you choose for a solid color fabric? For a plaid? ______________

____

____

____

3. What are the characteristics of a quality thread? ___________________________________

____

____

4. Identify three kinds of threads and tell when each should be used. ____________________

____

____

____

____

5. What is the difference between a separating zipper and a two-way zipper? ______________

____

____

6. Why might a shank button be a good choice for heavy fabrics? ________________________

____

____

(continued on next page)

Clothing: Fashion, Fabrics & Construction Student Activity Manual
Copyright © by The McGraw-Hill Companies, Inc. All rights reserved.

Name____ Date________________ Class _______________

7. Why are tapes and trims added to garments? _______________________________________

____

____

8. What is ribbing and how is it used? ____

____

____

____

9. For what application would woven elastic and braided elastic both be appropriate?_________

____

10. Why is some interfacing called "fusible"? ____

____

____

11. How should you determine what weight of interfacing is appropriate for a specific fabric?

____

____

____

____

12. How is lining added to a garment? ____

____

____

13. How do fusible webs work?____

____

____

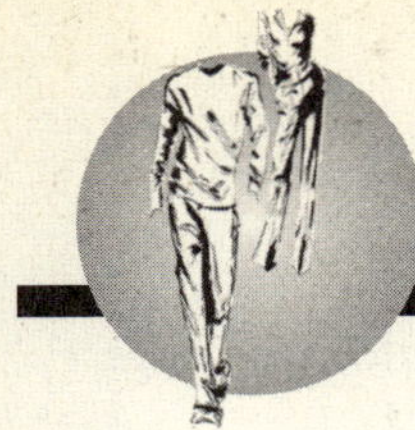

Advice About Notions

Directions: Imagine that you work in public relations for a chain of fabric stores. One of your duties is to write a customer newsletter. Your topic for the monthly "I've got a notion" feature is zippers. Complete the article below by describing types of zippers. Then respond to e-mail and letters received from readers in the publication's "Reader Mailbag" section. Use an additional sheet of paper if necessary.

I've got a notion….

Check out our full line of zippers for every purpose. Our friendly sales staff can help you select just the right type for your sewing project. All zippers are 20% off this month! Here's a rundown of what's available.

____

____

____

____

____

____

____

____

____

____

Reader Mailbag

1. My neighbor has developed vision problems, so she has given me her treasured sewing basket. There is some thread that would be a perfect match for some knit shirts I am making, but I am not sure what kind it is. Do you think I should use it? It is on wooden spools.

____

____

____

(continued on next page)

Lesson 3
Activity (continued)

2. I want a really sleek look for a dress I am sewing for a formal wedding reception. What would you suggest for the zipper?

____

____

3. Is it okay to reuse buttons? I like my clothes to have a retro look and I have found some great buttons on old clothes in the attic. Some are kind of large and have a metal hook in the back. What would be a good project to use them for?

____

____

____

4. Help! I have almost completed a pair of dress pants for my six-year-old nephew and he seems to have grown overnight. There is really not enough fabric for a hem. I hope there's a solution.

____

____

____

5. My grandmother needs some new blouses—nothing that must be pulled over her head though. She lives in an assisted-care facility but tries to be as independent as possible. Do you have any suggestions?

____

____

____

6. Last summer I made some shorts with a waistband that seemed flimsy and always rolled over. What can I do to have a nice, crisp waistband this time?

____

____

____

7. I prefer the look of a lined jacket, but the idea of making one is intimidating to me. What do I need to know?

____

____

____

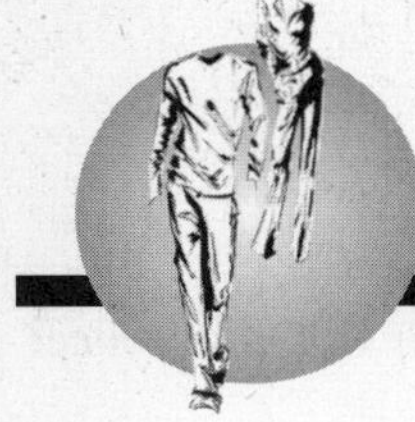

Using a Sewing Machine

Directions: As you read the lesson, answer the following questions. Later you can use this study guide to review for the Part 2 Handbook test.

1. Why is a ballpoint needle especially good for knits? _______________________________________

____

____

2. How is a leather needle designed for its purpose? _______________________________________

____

____

3. Which size needle is finer, a 9 or a 14? How do you know this? _____________________________

____

____

____

4. Why must the take-up lever move up and down as you sew? _________________________________

____

____

____

5. What is the function of the tension discs? ____

____

____

6. What do the numbers on the stitch-length control indicate? ________________________________

____

____

____

(continued on next page)

Lesson 4
Study Guide (continued)

7. How do a basting stitch and a reinforcement stitch compare in length? What is the reason for this difference?

____

____

____

____

8. How does a properly balanced stitch appear? __________________________________

____

____

9. Why is correct pressure between the presser foot and feed dogs important to sewing a secure seam?

____

____

10. Identify three possible causes for skipped stitches in a seam. ____________________

____

____

____

11. Why is the zipper foot useful for attaching zippers? ____________________________

____

____

12. How would you remove lint from a sewing machine? ____________________________

____

____

13. Why might you choose a computerized machine? Why might you not? ______________

____

____

____

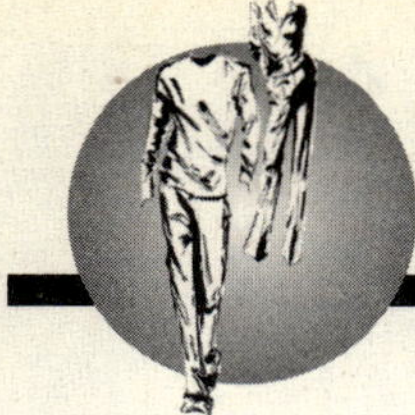

Parts of a Sewing Machine

Directions: Read the functions of the sewing machine components described below. In the space provided, write the name of the correct part. No part will be used more than once. Some parts will not be used.

Bobbin	Needle	Stitch-pattern control
Bobbin case	Needle clamp	Stitch-width control
Bobbin winder	Presser foot	Take-up lever
Feed dog	Reverse button	Tension control
Foot or knee control	Spool pins	Thread guides
Hand wheel	Stitch-length control	Throat or needle plate

_______________________________ 1. Helps guide upper thread from spool to needle without tangling.

_______________________________ 2. Controls movement of the take-up lever; can be turned by hand to raise or lower the needle.

_______________________________ 3. Teeth that move the fabric under the presser foot, advancing the fabric one stitch at a time.

_______________________________ 4. Holds the bottom thread.

_______________________________ 5. Holds spools of thread.

_______________________________ 6. Holds the fabric against the feed as you stitch.

_______________________________ 7. Regulates the tension of the tension discs on the needle thread.

_______________________________ 8. Control that allows you to stitch backwards.

_______________________________ 9. Regulates the starting, running, and stopping of the machine.

_______________________________ 10. Controls the amount of thread pulled from the top spool for each stitch; moves up and down as you stitch.

_______________________________ 11. Regulates the width of zigzag stitching and positions the needle for straight stitching.

_______________________________ 12. Regulates the length of the stitch.

_______________________________ 13. Located directly under the needle; usually has guidelines to help maintain straight stitching.

_______________________________ 14. Pierces the fabric with the upper thread to form stitches.

_______________________________ 15. Regulates the selection of different stitches.

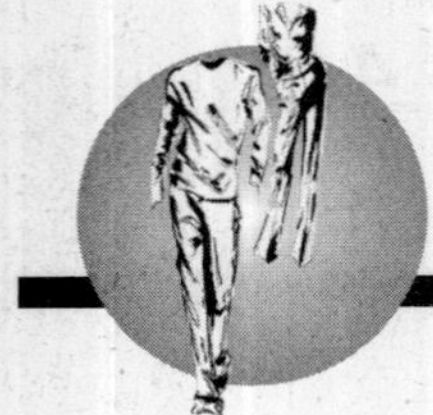

Sewing Machine Knowledge

Lesson 4
Activity

Directions: Decide whether you agree or disagree with each statement below, placing a check mark in the appropriate box. For any statement that you disagree with, cross out the incorrect part. On the line provided, write substitute words that make the statement accurate.

Agree   Disagree

☐   ☐   1. Replace sewing machine needles when they become dull, bent, or rough.

____

☐   ☐   2. Ballpoint needles have a tip that is filled with a small amount of ink.

____

☐   ☐   3. A low needle number, such as 11, is designed for thick, heavyweight fabric.

____

☐   ☐   4. Bobbins hold the bottom thread in sewing machines.

____

☐   ☐   5. Tension discs should be threaded after threading the take-up lever.

____

☐   ☐   6. After raising the bobbin thread, pull the thread ends toward the back of the machine to prevent tangling.

____

☐   ☐   7. Setting the stitch-length control to 3 means that you will sew three stitches per inch.

____

☐   ☐   8. The presser foot of the sewing machine holds the fabric against the feed dog.

____

☐   ☐   9. If the needle breaks while you are sewing, you may have too many layers of fabric.

____

☐   ☐   10. To avoid oil stains on fabric, do not add oil to your sewing machine.

____

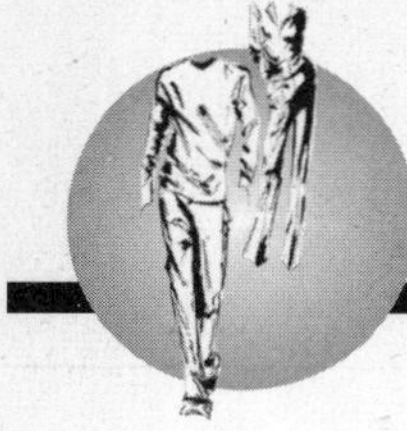

Using a Serger

Directions: As you read the lesson, answer the following questions. Later you can use this study guide to review for the Part 2 Handbook test.

1. How can you use both a serger and a conventional machine to sew clothes with ready-to-wear features?

____

____

____

____

____

____

2. What thread penetrates the fabric in a serged stitch? ____

3. Why are retractable knives a useful serger feature? ____

____

____

4. What advantages does a differential feed offer? ____

____

____

____

5. What is the safety stitch and what is its purpose? ____

____

____

____

____

(continued on next page)

Lesson 5
Study Guide (continued)

6. What are three possible uses of the rolled hemstitch?________________________________

____

____

____

7. When do you need to adjust serger tension to maintain a balanced stitch? ______________

____

____

8. Refer to Fig. 5-16. Identify problems that may result from using a dull or bent needle. ______________

____

____

____

9. What special threads can be used with sergers? _________________________________

____

____

____

10. How can you determine which tension dial controls each thread?________________________

____

____

____

11. Give two general guidelines for serger care. ____________________________________

____

____

____

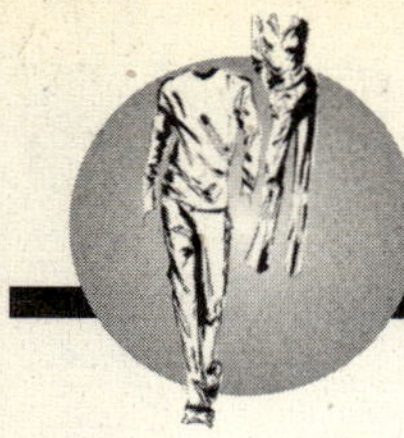

Parts of a Serger

Directions: Can you identify the parts of a serger? On the lines provided, write the names of the numbered parts shown in the illustrations below.

1. _______________________________
2. _______________________________
3. _______________________________
4. _______________________________
5. _______________________________
6. _______________________________
7. _______________________________

8. _______________________________
9. _______________________________
10. _______________________________
11. _______________________________
12. _______________________________
13. _______________________________
14. _______________________________
15. _______________________________

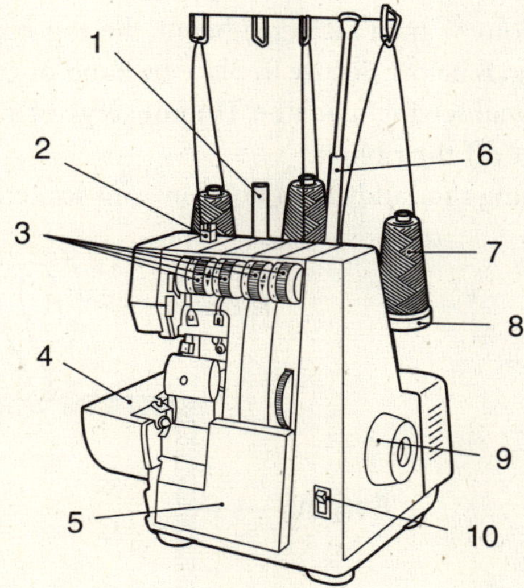

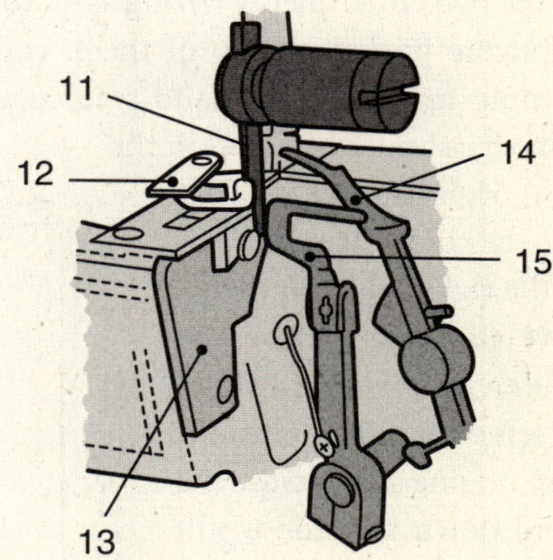

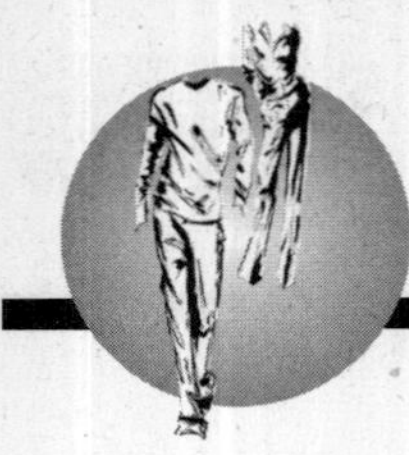

Serging Practice

Directions: To practice your serging skills, follow the directions below to create a simple locker caddy.

Locker Caddy

Equipment and Materials

- Sturdy, woven fabric, approximately 12 × 18 inches (30.5 × 46 cm)
- Ribbon, any type, 8 inches (20.5 cm)
- Serger
- Shears
- Ruler

- Tailor's chalk or marking pen
- Straight pins
- Liquid seam sealant (optional)

Procedure

1. On a single layer of fabric, mark two 12 × 6-inch (30.5 × 15-cm) rectangles and a 5 × 6-inch (12.5 × 15-cm) rectangle. The 12-inch (30.5-cm) side should be on the vertical grain of the fabric. Cut out the three pieces.

2. Serge one 6-inch (15-cm) side of the smaller piece. This will be the upper edge of the pocket.

3. Place the two larger pieces **wrong** sides together. Position the pocket on top of these, **right** side out, lining up the bottom and side edges. The serged edge should be about in the middle. See **Fig. A** below. Pin.

4. Serge the bottom edge first from the right side. **Important: remove the pins before they get near the serger blade.** Then serge from the bottom to the top on one side, across the top and down the side to the bottom.

5. Secure all thread chains by knotting or using liquid seam sealant. Trim off thread chains.

6. Fold the 8-inch (20.5-cm) length of ribbon in half and pin the cut ends to the center of the top of the locker caddy. Extend the loop above the caddy; the ends of the ribbon should extend about ⅝ inch (1.5 cm) below the top edge. See **Fig. B** below. Secure in place by hand or conventional sewing machine. **Do not serge** or you will cut off the ribbon.

7. Hang the caddy on a hook in your locker.

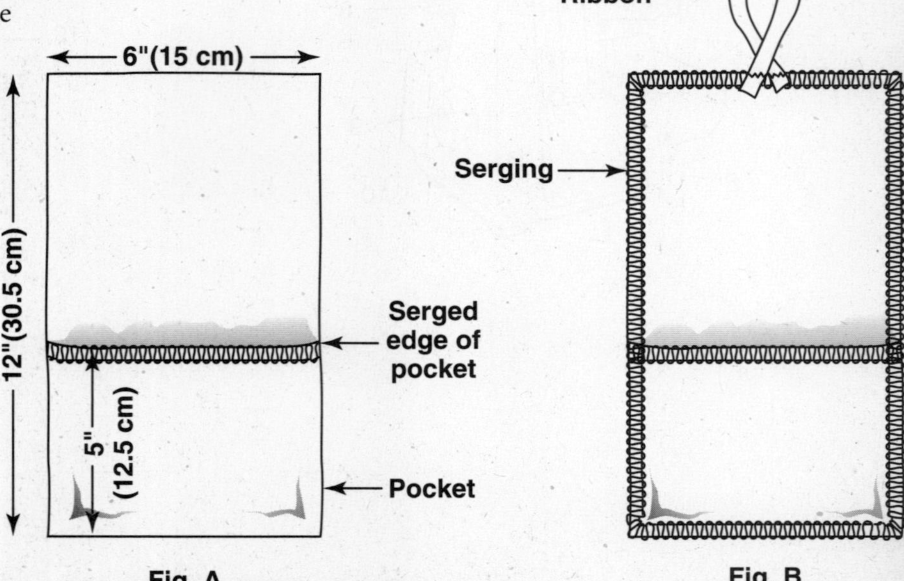

Fig. A

Fig. B

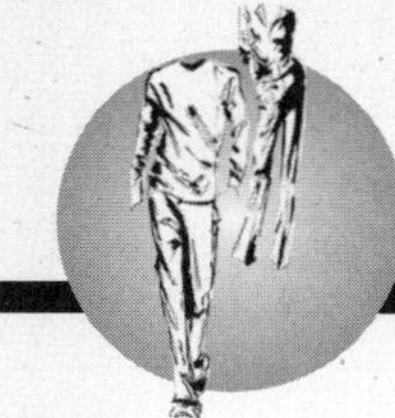

Identifying Sewing Equipment

Directions: As you read the lesson, answer the following questions. Later you can use this study guide to review for the Part 2 Handbook test.

1. What are the six basic purposes of sewing equipment? _____________________________________

____

2. What is a sewing gauge used for? ____

____

3. For what tasks is a transparent ruler especially useful? ____________________________________

____

____

____

4. Describe three uses for pins in sewing. ____

____

____

____

5. What kind of pin is best for working with a knitted fabric? _________________________________

6. Why do shears have bent handles? ____

____

7. What is the purpose of pinking shears? Would you use them if you are using a serger for your project? Why or why not?

____

____

____

____

____

(continued on next page)

Lesson 6
Study Guide (continued)

8. List four tools used to mark fabric.____

____

9. What is one advantage of using a fabric marking pen? ___________________________

____

____

10. How are glue sticks and basting tape similar?_________________________________

____

____

11. What are two uses for a press cloth? ____

____

____

____

12. What pieces of equipment are specially made for pressing curved areas of a garment?___________

____

13. Give three tips for organizing a sewing box. __________________________________

____

____

____

____

14. What may result from ironing over pins? _____________________________________

____

Clothing: Fashion, Fabrics & Construction Student Activity Manual

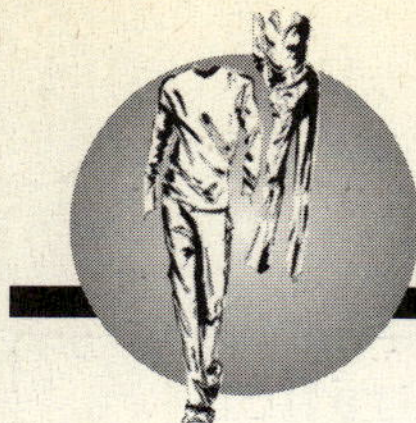

Identifying Tools and Supplies

Directions: Complete the chart below by providing the missing information in the boxes. When writing descriptions, specify the purpose of the tool or supply.

Name of Tool or Supply	Description	Illustration
1.		
2.		
3.		
4.		
5.		

(continued on next page)

Lesson 6
Activity (continued)

Name of Tool or Supply	Description	Illustration
6.		
7.		
8.		
9.		
10.		

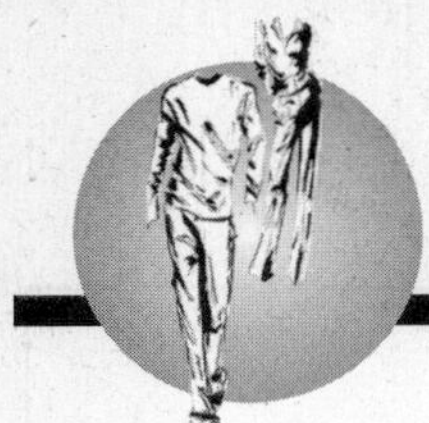

Safety Rules

Directions: This activity will help you prepare for sewing safely at school and elsewhere. Select the answer that best completes each statement below. Write the letter on the line at the left. Then on the next page complete the writing assignment described under "Safety Awareness," and sign and date the safety contract with your teacher.

_______ 1. Protect yourself while operating a sewing machine by ___.
  A. wearing lightweight goggles
  B. not leaning too close in case the needle breaks
  C. placing a thimble on your thumb
  D. wearing appropriate clothing

_______ 2. When you are just learning to operate a sewing machine, you should ___.
  A. be sure to loosen the tension
  B. choose a setting for small stitches
  C. secure the fabric you are sewing by pinning at 1-inch intervals
  D. operate the machine at a slow speed

_______ 3. It is permissible to use pins while serging only if ___.
  A. the serger is an industrial machine
  B. pins are placed an inch away from the fabric's edge
  C. pins are made of titanium
  D. you are very experienced

_______ 4. Instead of pinning fabric when using a serger, you may ___.
  A. use a glue stick
  B. sew with an eight-thread machine
  C. use two needles
  D. hold the fabric together with your fingers

_______ 5. While pinning a project together, do **not** place pins in ___.
  A. a magnetic pincushion
  B. their original container
  C. your clothes or mouth
  D. a wrist pincushion

_______ 6. Hand scissors to a classmate by ___.
  A. extending the handle first
  B. extending scissors with open blades facing you
  C. extending the closed blade first
  D. sliding scissors along the floor or counter

_______ 7. When you set your scissors down while working, you should ___.
  A. put them back in their protective case
  B. place them near the edge of the sewing machine
  C. close the blades
  D. hang them from string by the machine

_______ 8. All of the following sewing tools are very sharp, **except** ___.
  A. needles
  B. rotary cutters
  C. dressmaker's shears
  D. tracing wheels

(continued on next page)

Lessons 4, 5, 6
Activity (continued)

Safety Awareness

Sewing is an enjoyable pastime, but it can be dangerous when equipment is used incorrectly. Explain below what injuries can occur while sewing and why they may happen. List precautions you will take to avoid injury while sewing.

____

____

____

____

____

____

____

____

____

____

____

____

____

Safety Contract

As a student enrolled in (course name)____

at (school name)____,

I understand the sewing safety precautions explained to me and realize that I have the responsibility to help prevent injuries in the classroom.

Student's Signature ___________________________________ Date _______________

Teacher's Signature ___________________________________ Date _______________

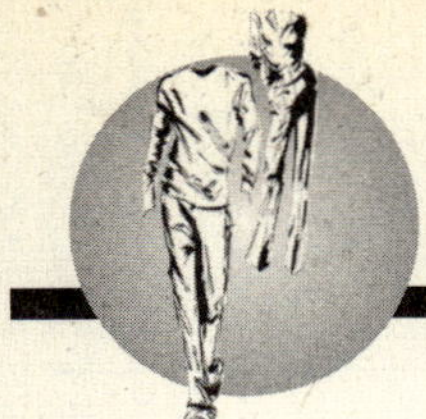

Understanding Patterns

Lesson 7
Study Guide

Directions: As you read the lesson, answer the following questions. Later you can use this study guide to review for the Part 3 Handbook test.

1. Give two guidelines for organizing a project before actually beginning to sew. _________________

____

____

2. Why should you press a garment after each construction step? __________________________

____

____

____

3. What are the three parts of a pattern? ____

____

4. What are four things you can learn by reading the front of a pattern envelope? ____________

____

____

____

____

____

5. How does a cutting layout help you organize pattern pieces?____________________________

____

____

____

____

____

(continued on next page)

Lesson 7
Study Guide (continued)

6. How are pattern pieces marked to make sewing easier? ___________________________________

____

____

____

____

7. When preparing a pattern, how can you help ensure that you use only the pattern pieces you need?

____

____

____

____

8. How do you use the grain line to place pattern pieces on grain? ___________________________

____

____

9. How can you tell where to sew garment pieces together if a pattern piece is not marked with a seam line?

____

____

10. What is the difference between "place on fold" and "fold line" marked on a pattern piece? _____________

____

____

____

____

11. How can you be sure to use the size you want when using a multisized pattern? __________________

____

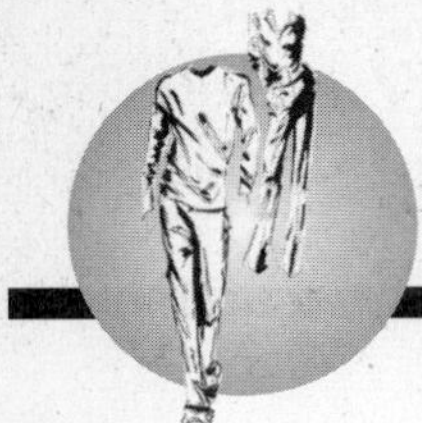

Using Patterns

Directions: What if you were missing part of your pattern? It would be nearly impossible to complete the project! The pattern envelope, guide sheet, and tissue pattern pieces are all vital components of a pattern. Using the codes shown below, indicate where you would expect to find the pattern information and features listed. Then respond to the hypothetical situation that follows.

PE: Pattern Envelope   **GS:** Guide Sheet   **PP:** Pattern Pieces

_______ 1. Cutting layouts

_______ 2. Photo of finished projects

_______ 3. Amount of fabric needed

_______ 4. Notches

_______ 5. Average time required to complete project

_______ 6. Step-by-step directions

_______ 7. Cutting lines for multisized patterns

_______ 8. General sewing directions

_______ 9. Back view of garments

_______ 10. Dots

_______ 11. Designation as "easy to sew"

_______ 12. Fabric key

_______ 13. Adjustment lines

_______ 14. Required notions

_______ 15. Placement lines

Angela sewed her favorite pants from an easy-to-sew pattern. When she had trouble fitting the tissue pattern pieces back in the envelope, she placed them in a large mailing envelope instead and discarded the pattern envelope. Identify at least three obstacles Angela will encounter when she tries to sew the shirt that is offered as View A. Do you think Angela will be able to sew the shirt? Explain. How could Angela have avoided these problems?

____

____

____

____

____

____

____

____

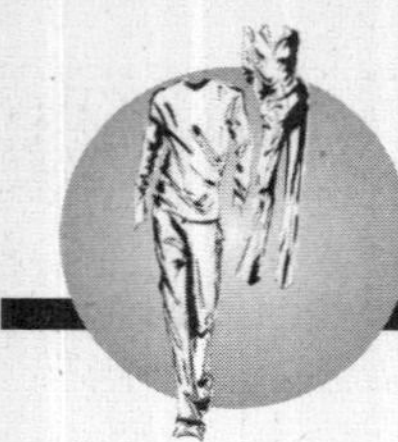

Identifying Pattern Markings

Directions: Study these pattern pieces for the front and sleeve of a fitted V-neck shirt. Identify the numbered symbols on the lines below.

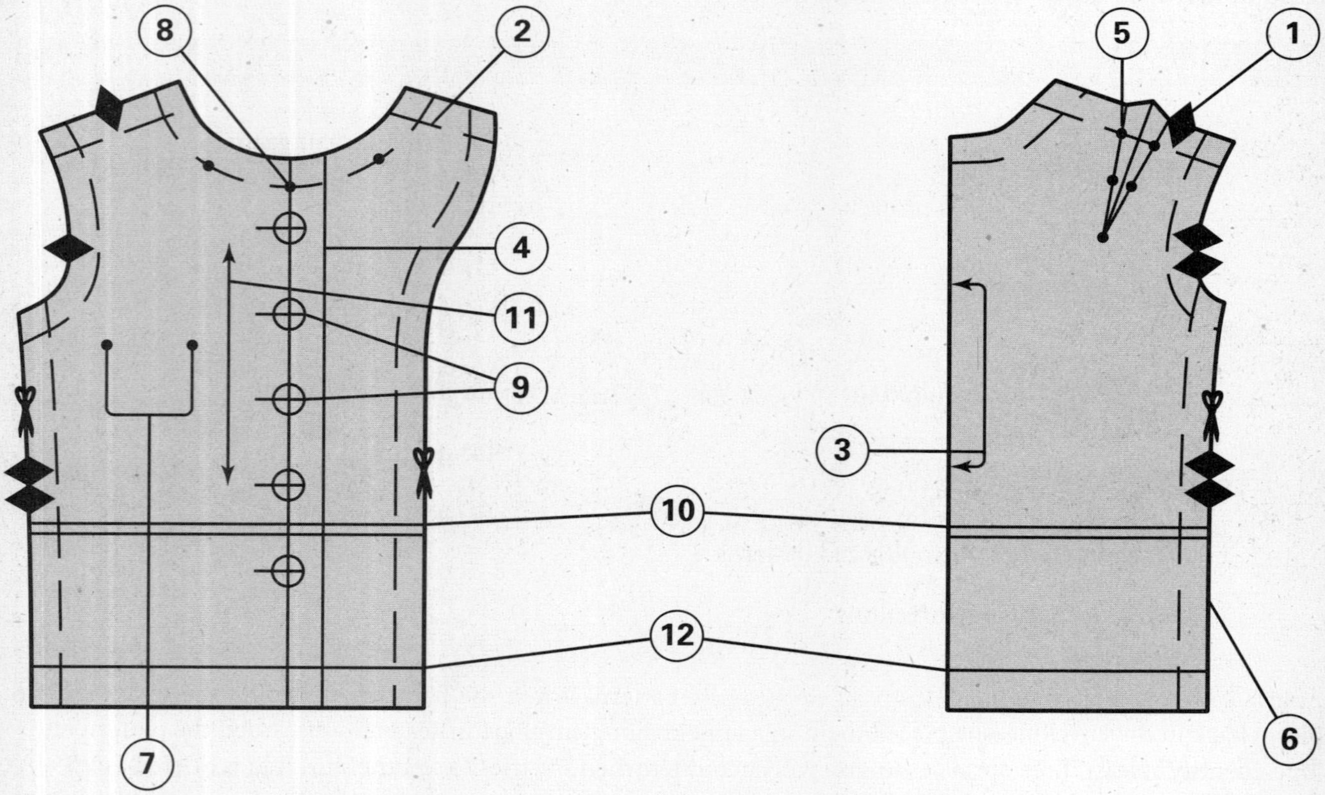

1. _______________________

2. _______________________

3. _______________________

4. _______________________

5. _______________________

6. _______________________

7. _______________________

8. _______________________

9. _______________________

10. _______________________

11. _______________________

12. _______________________

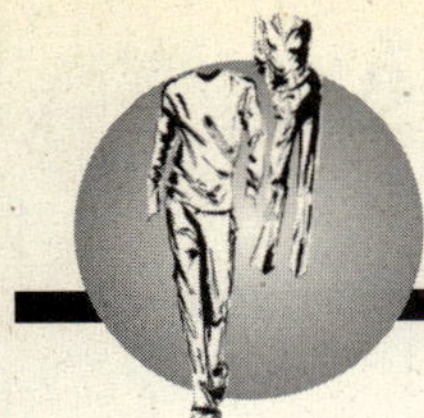

Adjusting a Pattern

Lesson 8
Study Guide

Directions: As you read the lesson, answer the following questions. Later you can use this study guide to review for the Part 3 Handbook test.

1. Why are pattern pieces usually larger than the body measurements of the size they fit? _______________

____

____

2. How can it be useful to make a chart comparing your measurements with those listed on the pattern envelope?

____

____

3. When measuring pattern pieces, what areas should not be included in your measurement? _______________

____

4. How can even a minor error in measuring cause problems when adjusting a pattern?_______________

____

____

5. Summarize the main steps to lengthening a pattern piece at an adjustment line. _______________

____

____

____

6. What is the largest amount that a garment can be adjusted at the side seams? What must be done for larger adjustments?

____

____

7. How do you decrease pattern width at a waistline? At the hipline? _______________________________

____

____

____

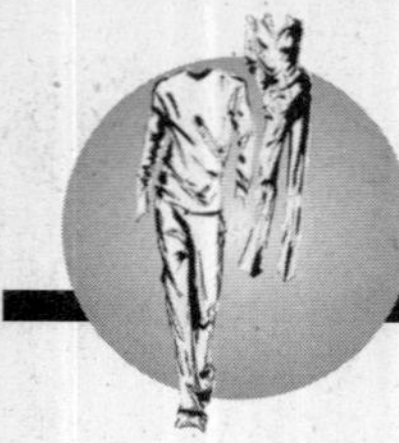

Pattern Adjustments

Directions: Multisized patterns for shorts are shown below with three sizes—1, 2, and 3. Suppose you are following size 2. On pattern A, mark in pencil where you might draw a new cutting line to get more room in the waist and less in the hips. On pattern B, mark cutting lines for a smaller waist and larger hips. Then answer the questions that follow.

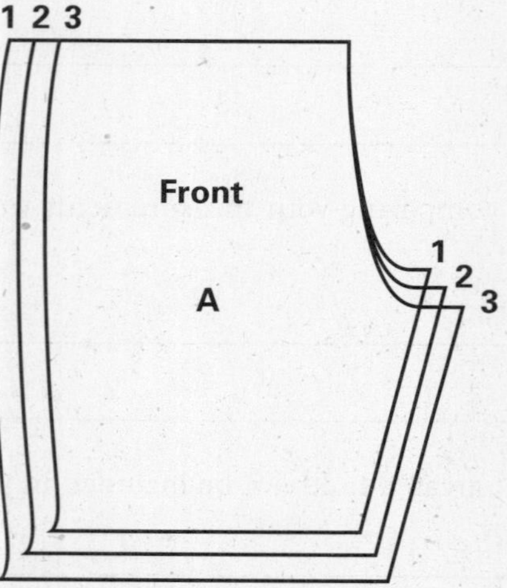

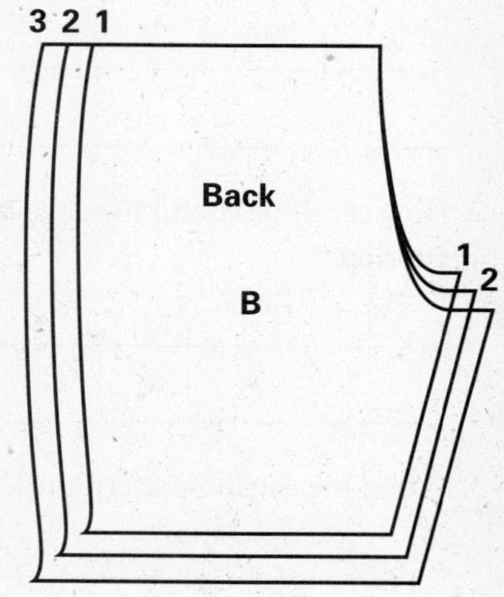

1. How much wearing ease would you expect that the designer built into this garment at the waistline? At the hips?

____

2. If you wanted the waist to be 1 inch (2.5 cm) larger, how much would you increase each side seam? Why?

____

____

3. If you wanted longer shorts, describe how you would lengthen the lower edge of the pattern.

____

____

____

4. For properly fitting clothes, what advantages do you have when sewing garments rather than buying them ready-made?

____

____

____

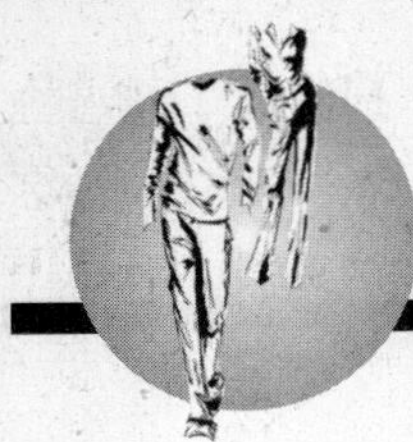

Lesson 9
Study Guide

Preparing Fabric

Directions: As you read the lesson, answer the following questions. Later you can use this study guide to review for the Part 3 Handbook test.

1. How can you straighten uneven ends of a woven fabric if you can't see the crosswise yarns? _______________

____

____

2. How can you straighten the ends of knitted fabrics? _______________

____

____

3. Why is it a good idea to preshrink fabric? _______________

____

____

4. What is the main difference between the lengthwise grain and crosswise grain? _______________

____

____

____

5. How would you cut fabric to give a garment the most stretch? _______________

____

6. How can you see whether a piece of fabric is straight? _______________

____

____

____

7. Why is it important to know whether a center fold can be pressed out of a piece of fabric? _______________

____

____

____

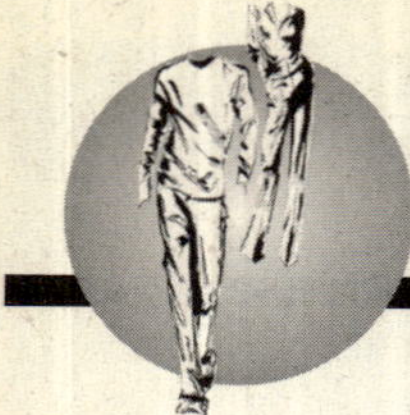

Fabric Preparation Checklist

Directions: There are typically four steps involved in preparing fabric for a sewing project. Follow the steps below to prepare your fabric, answering the questions at each step.

STEP 1   Straighten fabric ends.

1. Why is this step necessary? ____

____

2. Which method is best for your fabric? Why? _______________________________

____

STEP 2   Preshrink fabric.

3. Which method will you use? Why? _______________________________________

____

4. What risks do you take if you omit this step? _______________________________

____

STEP 3   Straighten fabric grain.

5. How can you check whether fabric needs to be straightened? Whether your fabric is off-grain? _________

____

____

6. Why might you be unable to straighten the grain? ___________________________

____

STEP 4   Press fabric.

7. Why is this step necessary? ____

____

8. What should you do if you're unable to press out the center fold?________________

____

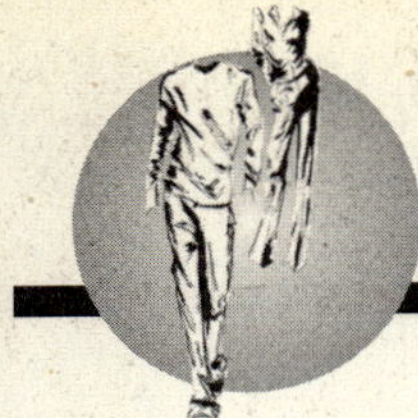

Laying Out a Pattern

Directions: As you read the lesson, answer the following questions. Later you can use this study guide to review for the Part 3 Handbook test.

1. What precaution should you take when working with a fabric with a similar right and wrong side? Why?

   ____

   ____

   ____

2. Why is the right side of the fabric usually folded inward for layout and cutting? _______________

   ____

   ____

3. What additional step do napped fabrics need when folded crosswise? Why? _______________

   ____

   ____

   ____

4. Why wouldn't a sofa be a good surface for a pattern layout and cutting? _______________

   ____

5. Which pattern pieces should be pinned on your fabric first? Which should be pinned after those?

   ____

   ____

6. What should you do to cut two pieces of fabric from one pattern piece on a single fabric layer?

   ____

7. What points should you check after laying out pattern pieces? _______________

   ____

8. Explain how to lay out pattern pieces for a fabric that has uneven vertical stripes. _______________

   ____

   ____

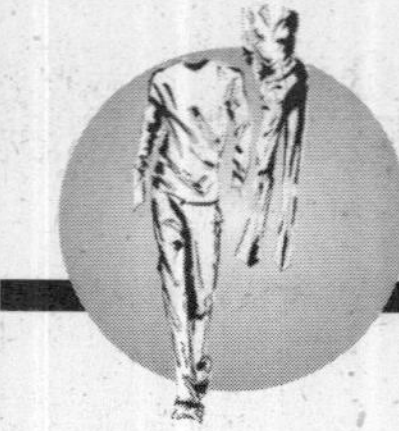

Pattern Layout Procedure

Directions: Jenna is preparing to make a jumper. Follow the progress of her project and fill in the blanks with missing information.

____

1. Jenna identifies the right side of her knit fabric by stretching its crosswise cut edge. She knows it is the right side of the fabric because the edge __?__ to that side.

____

2. She marks the right side of the fabric with __?__.

____

3. She locates the correct cutting layout for her fabric width on the pattern guide sheet and __?__ it.

____

4. Jenna chooses the __?__-nap layout because her fabric has tulips with stems that should not be upside down.

____

5. Jenna folds the fabric __?__ side out so she can easily match the floral pattern.

____

6. After checking for straight grain, she pins the layers of fabric together at the __?__.

____

7. She works at a(n) __?__.

____

8. She starts by pinning the __?__ pattern piece at the fold.

____

9. The cutting layout for her jumper shows one pattern piece that is __?__ so she places it printed side down.

____

10. As she positions pattern pieces, she places pins at __?__ to the pattern edge.

____

11. In the corners, Jenna places pins __?__.

____

12. She tries to __?__ the floral pattern in the fabric by lining up notches on the jumper front with the corresponding notches for the back of the garment.

____

13. Jenna pins the jumper back pattern piece to the fabric and measures from the __?__ on the pattern piece to the edge of the fabric. She notes that the measurement at one end is ¼ inch (6 mm) more than at the other end.

____

14. Jenna shifts the pattern piece until the grain line is perfectly straight and then she __?__ it again.

____

15. Before __?__ the pattern pieces, she pauses to count them.

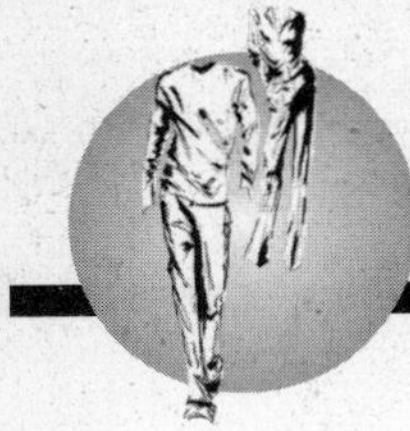

Cutting and Marking Fabric

Directions: As you read the lesson, answer the following questions. Later you can use this study guide to review for the Part 3 Handbook test.

1. What is directional cutting? ____

____

2. Why do you need to mark fabric pieces after cutting them out? _______________________

____

____

3. Why don't you need to mark seam allowances on fabric? _____________________________

____

4. Briefly explain how to mark fabric using a marking pen. _____________________________

____

____

____

5. How do you choose a color of tracing paper that leaves permanent marks? ______________

____

6. How are a tracing wheel and tracing paper used to mark symbols? _____________________

____

____

____

7. Summarize the procedure for using tailor's chalk. __________________________________

____

____

____

____

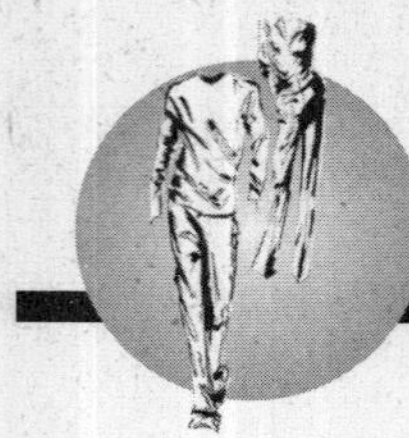

Cutting and Marking Methods

Lesson 11
Activity

Directions: On a piece of lightweight paper, copy the pattern piece below, enlarging it to at least double the size shown. Find a fabric scrap that is twice the size of your finished pattern piece. After gathering pins, bent-handled shears, tracing paper and wheel, tailor's chalk, and a fabric-marking pen, follow the directions below to practice pinning, cutting, and marking.

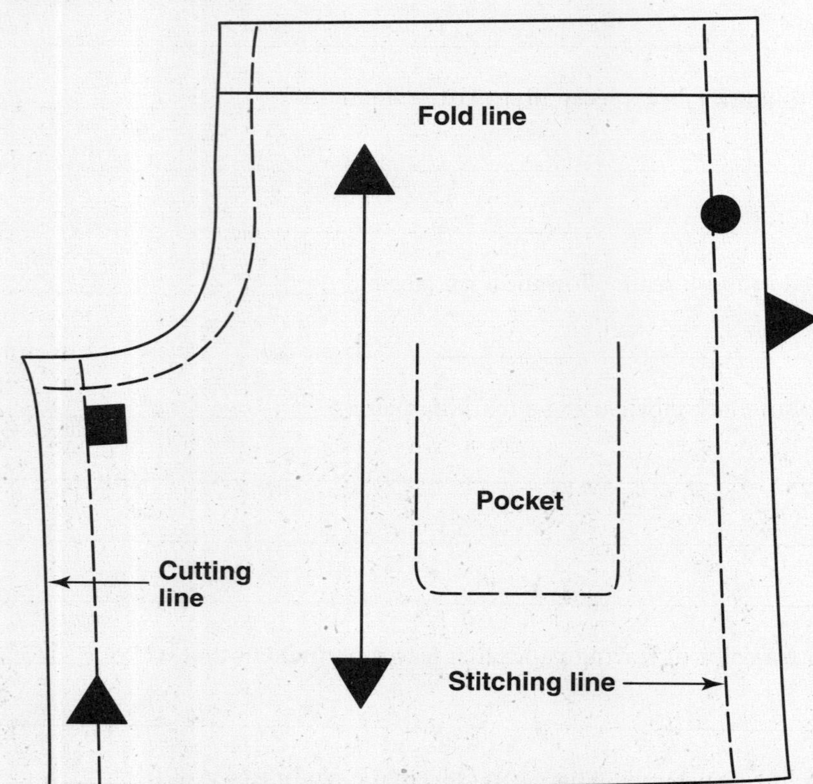

Pinning and Cutting	Marking
1. With right sides together, fold the fabric scrap in half, paying attention to the grain. 2. Place the copied pattern piece on the fabric. 3. Pin the pattern piece to the fabric. 4. Use bent-handled shears to cut out the pattern piece. Cut carefully around the notch. Do not remove the pins.	5. **Dot.** Use tracing paper and a tracing wheel to mark the dot on the wrong side of the fabric. 6. **Square.** Use tailor's chalk to mark the square on the wrong side of the fabric. Stick a pin through the pattern and fabric to help find the exact spot. 7. **Triangle.** Use a fabric-marking pen to mark the triangle symbol. 8. **Fold line.** Use a fabric-marking pen to mark the fold line. 9. **Pocket.** Choose any method above to mark the pocket location.

Clothing: Fashion, Fabrics & Construction Student Activity Manual

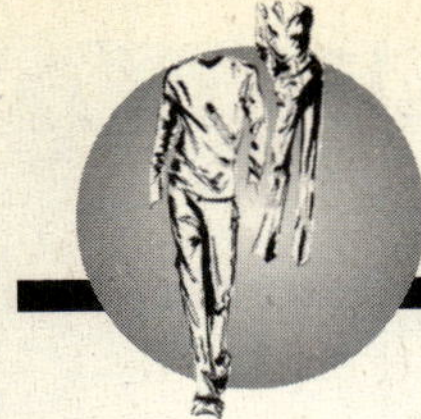

Stitching by Machine

Lesson 12
Study Guide

Directions: As you read the lesson, answer the following questions. Later you can use this study guide to review for the Part 4 Handbook test.

1. List the three stitch lengths from longest to shortest. _______________________________

____

2. When in the sewing process is staystitching added and what is its purpose? _______________

____

____

3. Why is understitching used? ____

____

____

4. How did the stitch-in-the-ditch get its name? ____

____

5. Explain what is meant by "chaining off." ____

____

6. What points should you look for when checking a machine before sewing? _________________

____

____

____

7. What are the steps in unit construction? ____

____

____

____

8. What tools are used for removing stitches? ____

____

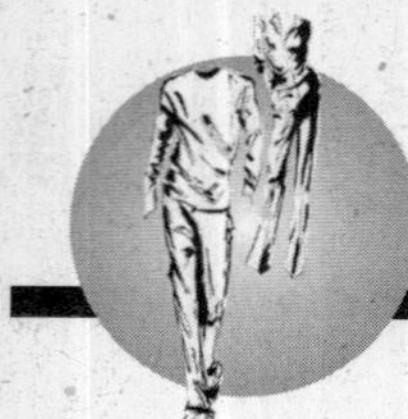

Identifying Machine Stitches

Lesson 12
Activity

Directions: Complete the sentences below by writing the name of the correct machine stitch in the blank to the left of each statement. Some machine stitches will be used more than once.

_______________________ 1. Straight lines of gold stitches down the legs of blue jeans show that __?__ can be both decorative and functional.

_______________________ 2. Even before joining garment pieces, you may need to use __?__ to help them keep their shape.

_______________________ 3. __?__ acts as an anchor, holding the ends of stitching lines fast.

_______________________ 4. When used on straight fabric grain, __?__ stitching may run either left to right or right to left.

_______________________ 5. With __?__ stitching, 10 to 12 stitches per inches (2 to 2.5 mm in length) is common.

_______________________ 6. As the name suggests, __?__ tightly holds fabric pieces close to the finished area.

_______________________ 7. Narrow __?__ stitches create a decorative effect; broader stitches are more functional.

_______________________ 8. __?__ stitching runs next to a seam line to secure fabric.

_______________________ 9. __?__ is often used to "hide" facing and bottom layers of fabric.

_______________________ 10. Garment parts held together only by __?__ stitches need more careful handling than completed parts.

_______________________ 11. Since diagonal lines add excitement to a design, __?__ stitching can be added for dramatic effect.

_______________________ 12. Tiny __?__ stitches add strength by securing only a few fabric yarns per stitch.

_______________________ 13. The length of __?__ stitching varies with the weight of the fabric.

_______________________ 14. Unless a pattern piece specifies a seam width of more or less than ⅝ inch (1.5 cm), you should use __?__ stitching.

_______________________ 15. __?__ is placed within the seam allowance of one piece of fabric.

_______________________ 16. Gathering fabric into ruffles is one use for __?__ stitches.

_______________________ 17. Add __?__ stitches to a seam before giving an area a close trim.

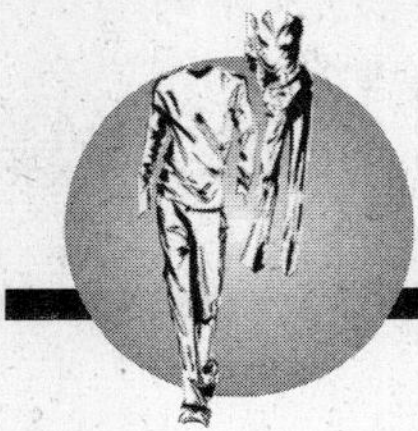

Stitching by Hand

Directions: As you read the lesson, answer the following questions. Later you can use this study guide to review for the Part 4 Handbook test.

1. When might you use hand stitching on a garment? _________________________________

____

____

2. For hand sewing, a classmate unwinds a yard of thread and snaps it between his teeth. What problems might your classmate have using this thread?

____

____

3. Compare the purposes of even and uneven basting. _______________________________

____

____

4. What stitch would you use to prevent seam edges from raveling? ___________________

5. How is a blindstitch formed? Why is this stitch useful? ___________________________

____

____

____

6. For what situations might you use a catchstitch? _________________________________

____

7. How are blanket stitches made? ____

____

____

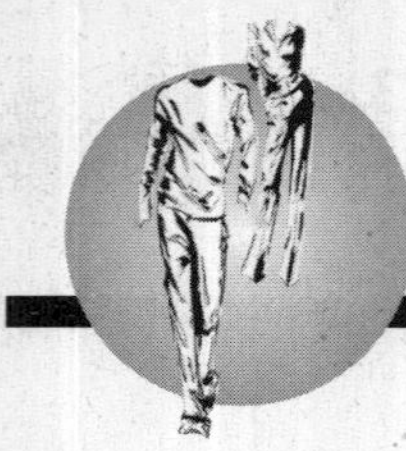

Identifying Hand Stitches

Lesson 13
Activity

Directions: Identify each of the nine stitches below and describe its use(s). Then cut out nine, 4-inch squares of fabric. Use these fabric squares to complete a sample of each stitch below. Mount your samples on paper and attach them to this activity sheet.

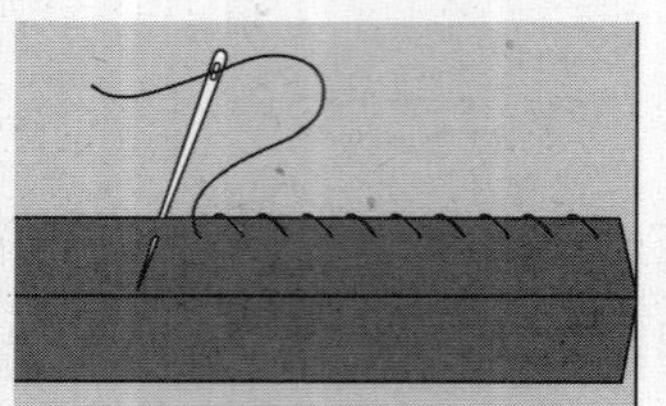

1.
Name: _______________________

Use(s): _______________________

____

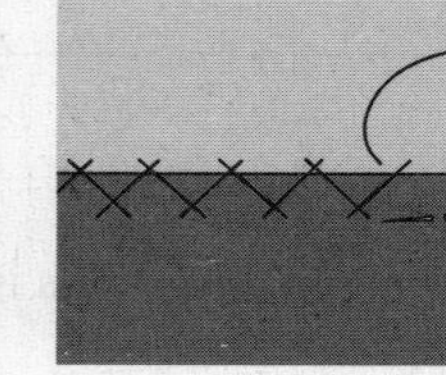

2.
Name: _______________________

Use(s): _______________________

____

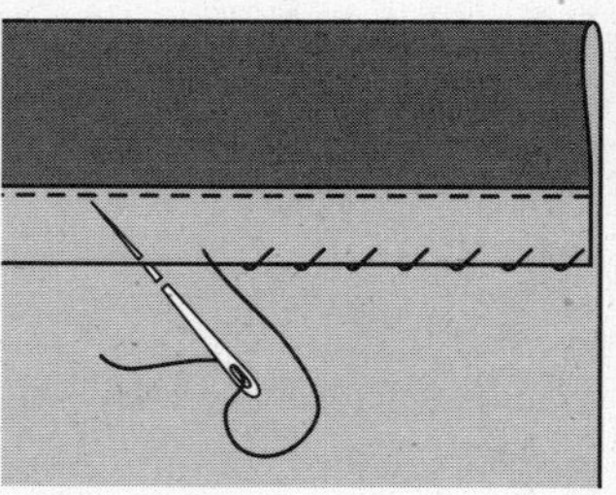

3.
Name: _______________________

Use(s): _______________________

____

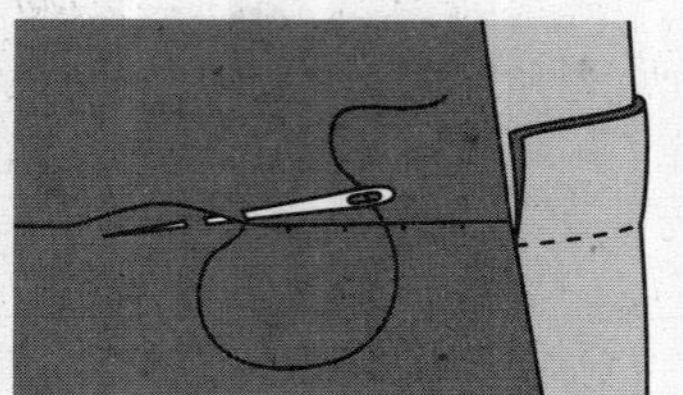

4.
Name: _______________________

Use(s): _______________________

____

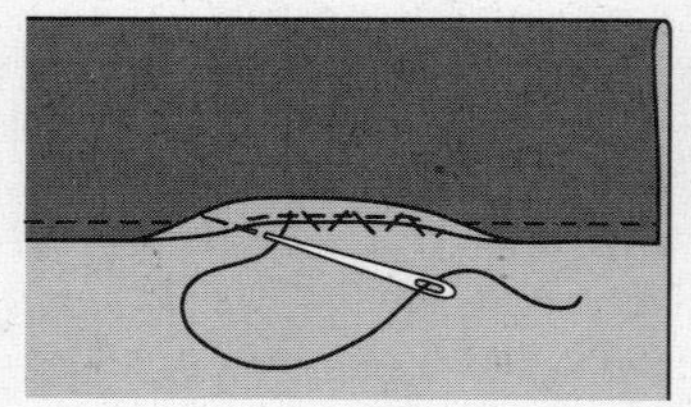

5.
Name: _______________________

Use(s): _______________________

____

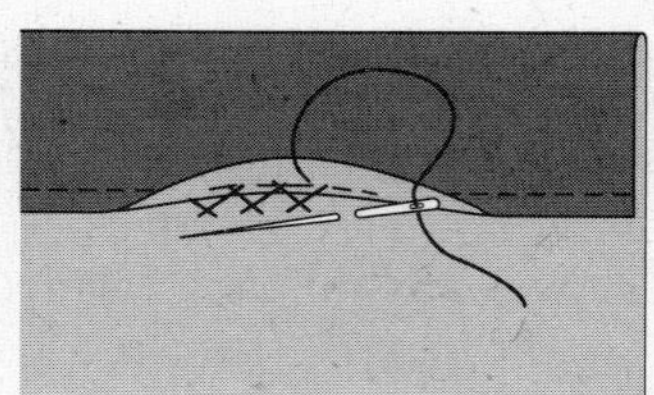

6.
Name: _______________________

Use(s): _______________________

____

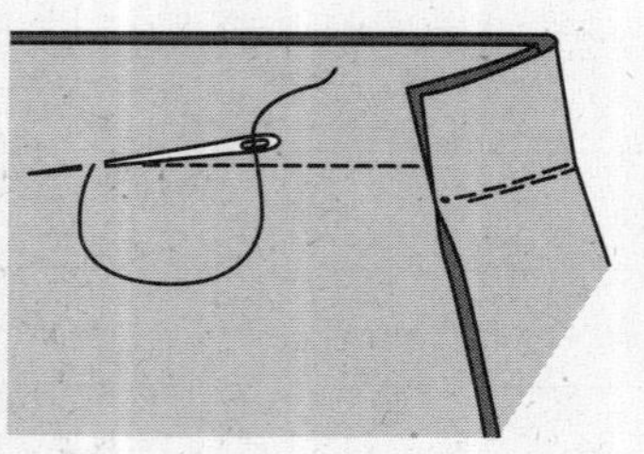

7.
Name: _______________________

Use(s): _______________________

____

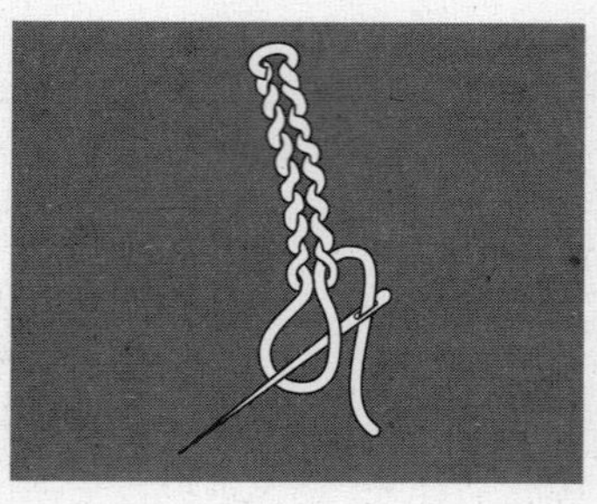

8.
Name: _______________________

Use(s): _______________________

____

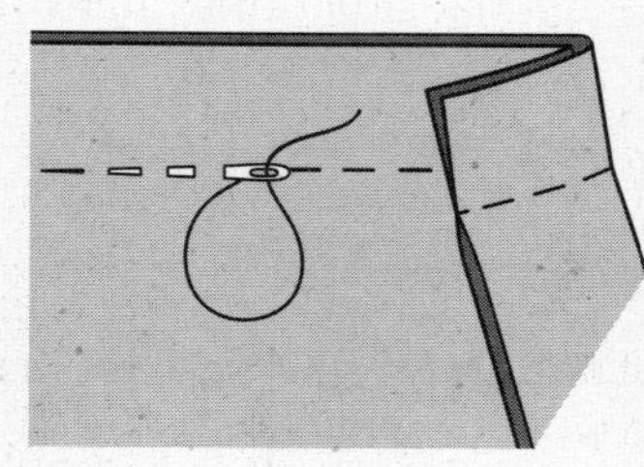

9.
Name: _______________________

Use(s): _______________________

____

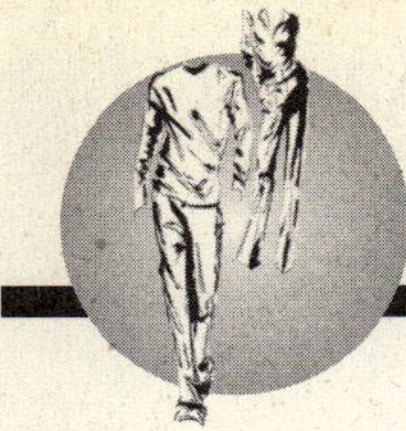

Pressing Fabric

Directions: As you read the lesson, answer the following questions. Later you can use this study guide to review for the Part 4 Handbook test.

1. Why is pressing rather than ironing better for garment construction? _______________________

____

____

____

2. What should you check for when "test pressing" a fabric before pressing the garment? _______________

____

____

____

____

3. When do you need to use a press cloth? Why? _______________________________________

____

____

4. Why are seams pressed flat before they're pressed open? _______________________________

____

____

5. In what order should you press the parts of an entire garment? _______________________

____

____

____

6. How can you prevent pressing a crease at the end of a dart? _______________________

____

____

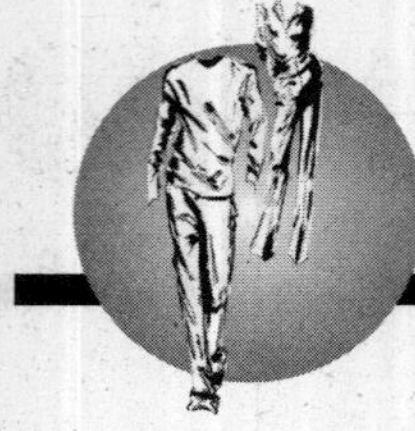

Pressing Pointers

Directions: Imagine that you are a guest on a talk show that is featuring special sewing segments this month. The studio audience has submitted the following questions about today's topic, pressing fabric. Write your responses on the lines provided.

1. I am never sure which temperature setting to use. How do I decide? ________________________

____

____

____

2. I ended up with the imprint of my iron on a skirt I was making. I do not think the iron was too hot. What could have happened?

____

____

3. Do you have any hints for pressing curved areas of a garment? ________________________

____

____

4. I know you are supposed to press seams open, but I do not like being able to see the press marks on the right side of the fabric. Is there a way to avoid this?

____

____

5. What is the best way to press a finished project? Is there a certain order to follow?

____

____

____

6. Is there a way to deal with a hem that has too much fullness?

____

____

____

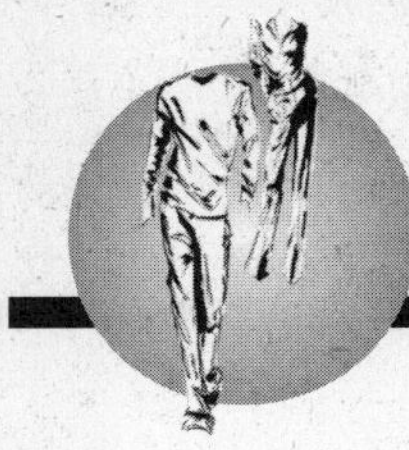

Making Darts

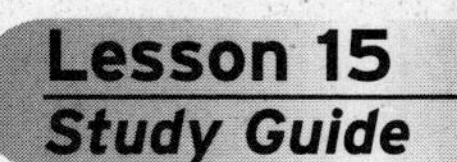

Directions: As you read the lesson, answer the following questions. Later you can use this study guide to review for the Part 4 Handbook test.

1. Why are darts made in garments? _______________________________________

____

____

2. How should darts be positioned in relation to the body? _______________________

____

____

____

3. In what direction are single darts stitched? Double-pointed darts? _______________

____

____

____

4. How do you make sharp points on darts? How do you handle the thread ends? _______

____

____

____

5. How do darts made using a serger compare to those made on a sewing machine? _______

____

____

6. How are the steps for making wider darts different from the steps for making small ones? _______

____

____

____

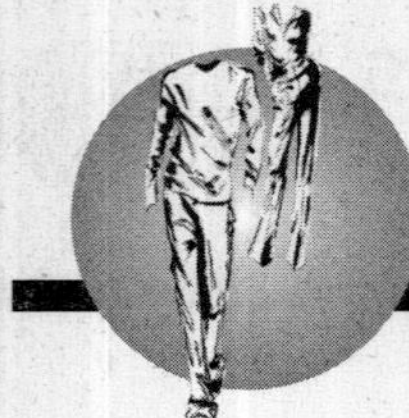

Quick Tips on Making Darts

Directions: Compile a list of do's and don'ts for making single-pointed darts by writing tips on the lines below. For the "do's" list, include how to fold fabric, the procedure for stitching a dart, what to do with thread ends, and how to press the dart. For the "don'ts" list, include points about backstitching, pressing, and using a serger.

Do's

1. ____

____

____

2. ____

____

____

3. ____

____

____

4. ____

____

____

____

Don'ts

1. ____

____

2. ____

____

3. ____

____

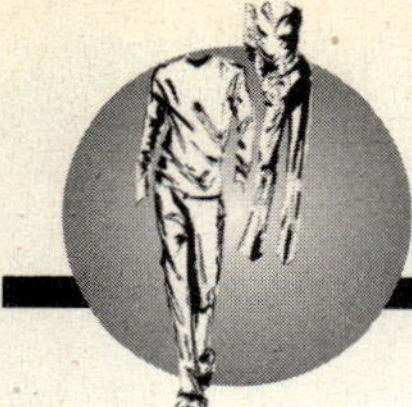

Gathering and Easing Fabric

Lesson 16
Study Guide

Directions: As you read the lesson, answer the following questions. Later you can use this study guide to review for the Part 4 Handbook test.

1. What are the three general steps for making gathers? ________________________________

   ____

   ____

2. How do you secure the bobbin threads after pulling a gathered section? ________________

   ____

3. What is the basic difference between making gathers with a serger and with a sewing machine?

   ____

   ____

4. What technique would you use to gather heavy fabric? ______________________________

   ____

   ____

5. How is shirring made?____

   ____

   ____

   ____

6. How is elasticized shirring made? ____

   ____

   ____

   ____

   ____

7. How is an eased seam different in appearance from a gathered seam? ___________________

   ____

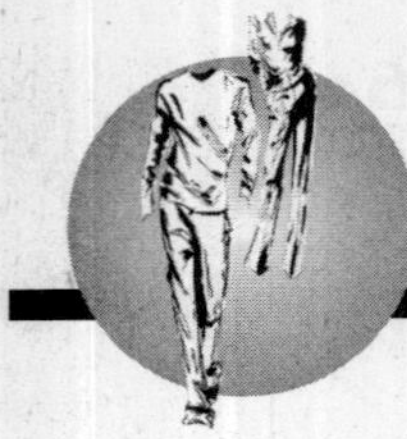

Controlling Fullness

Directions: Three techniques for controlling fullness are explained in text Lesson 16. Complete the statements below about these methods.

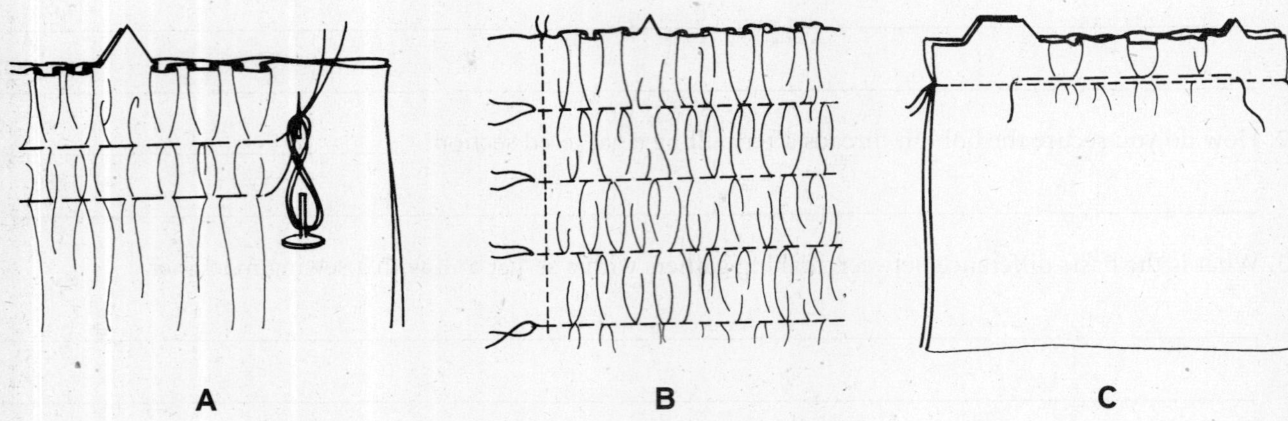

1. What are the three techniques for controlling fullness in the illustrations above?

   A: _________________________   B: _________________________   C: _________________________

2. Gathers are soft folds of fabric formed by pulling up _____________________________ rows of stitches to make the fabric fit into a smaller space.

3. Shirring is formed by several rows of____.

4. Easing is used when one edge of fabric is only slightly _____________________________ than the other.

5. When pressing gathers, start by pressing the _____________________________ flat.

6. _____________________________ should not be attempted with heavyweight fabric.

7. The beginning and end of a gathered area are marked on patterns by _____________________________.

8. The most common eased seam is a(n) _____________________________.

9. _____________________________ should not create any visible folds or gathers.

10. It takes _____________________________ yardage to create full gathers in lightweight fabrics than in heavier ones.

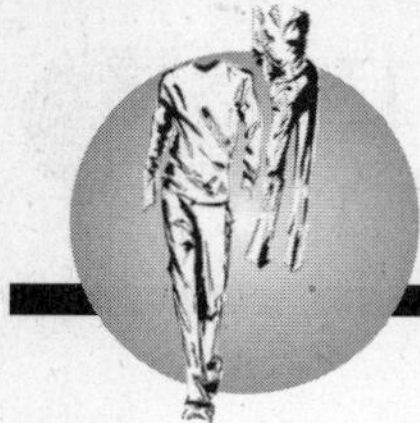

Sewing Plain Seams

Directions: As you read the lesson, answer the following questions. Later you can use this study guide to review for the Part 4 Handbook test.

1. How do you secure the beginning and end of a seam? _______________________________________

____

____

2. Why might you take diagonal stitches when turning a sharp point? _________________________

____

____

3. How would you trim the seam allowances of a very pointed corner? ________________________

____

____

____

4. How do you grade a seam allowance? ____

____

____

5. When is notching useful? ____

____

____

6. When are seam finishes added when using a sewing machine? When using a serger? __________

____

____

7. How would you make a secured, pinked seam finish? ___________________________________

____

____

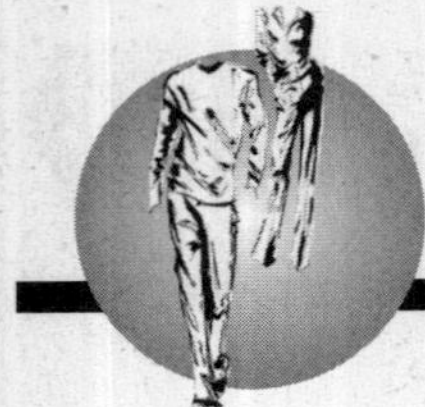

Practice with Plain Seams

Directions: To practice sewing plain seams, follow the directions below to create a four-patch quilt sample. Your class may want to sew all of the samples together to create one large top that can be finished as a quilt, or you could finish your sample as a small wall hanging or pillow.

Four-Patch Quilt Sample

Equipment and Materials
- Two contrasting fabric scraps, each at least 8 × 4 inches (20.5 × 10 cm)
- Ruler
- Tailor's chalk
- Thread
- Shears
- Sewing machine

Procedure

1. Mark two 4 × 4-inch (10 × 10-cm) squares on each piece of fabric. Be sure to have one side on the lengthwise grain of the fabric.
2. Cut out the four pieces.
3. Lay out the pieces on a flat surface, as illustrated below, with right sides up.

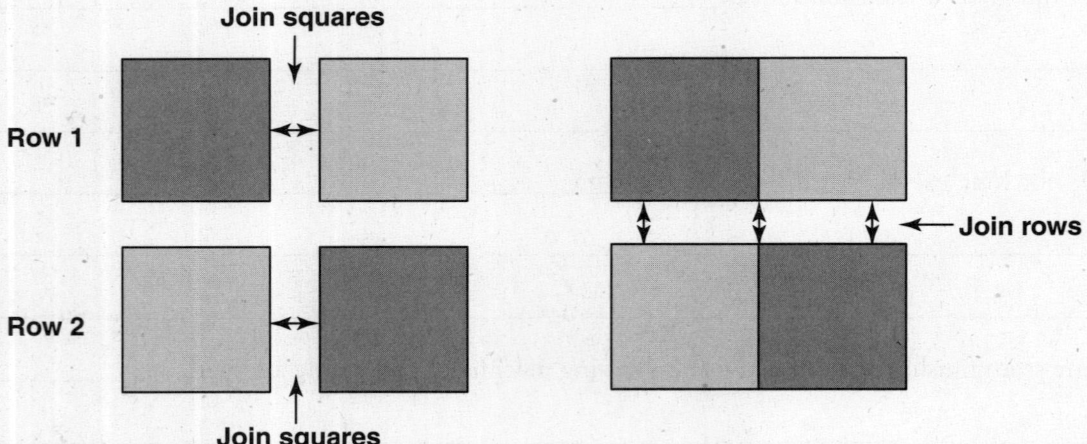

4. With **right** sides together, pin the two pieces in Row 1 together along one side, as shown by the arrows in the illustration. Be sure the raw edges are even. Repeat with the two pieces in Row 2.
5. On each row, machine-stitch the two pieces together, using a ⅝-inch (1.5-cm) seam allowance. Press the seams open.
6. With **right** sides together, pin Row 1 to Row 2 along one long side. Be sure to line up the seams sewn in Step 5.
7. Machine-stitch Row 1 and Row 2 together, using a ⅝-inch (1.5-cm) seam allowance. Press the seams open.

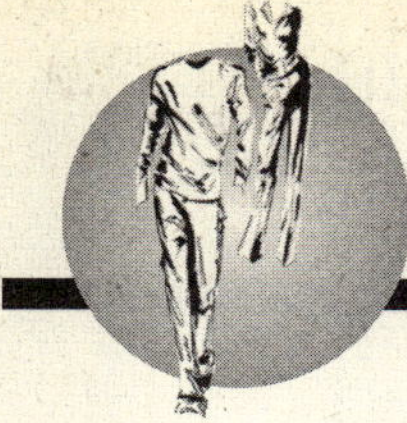

Applying Facings

Directions: As you read the lesson, answer the following questions. Later you can use this study guide to review for the Part 4 Handbook test.

1. Where are facings used? ____

____

2. What is another name for shaped facing? ____

____

3. When is bias facing most often used? ____

____

4. What helps you correctly position a facing against a garment before pinning? _________

____

5. Outline the main steps in attaching a facing. _____________________________________

____

____

____

____

6. What is one alternative to understitching a facing? ________________________________

____

____

7. When is a serger useful for attaching facings? Why? _______________________________

____

____

____

8. What are two general ways to fasten facings at seam allowances? _____________________

____

____

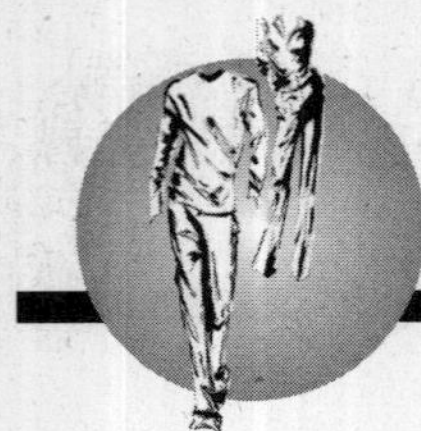

Checkup on Facings

Directions: Identify the two types of facings shown here. Then respond to the statements below by placing a plus (+) on the blank beside the true statements. Place a zero (0) on the blank next to the false statements. On a separate sheet of paper, rewrite each false statement to make it true. Attach your paper to this activity sheet.

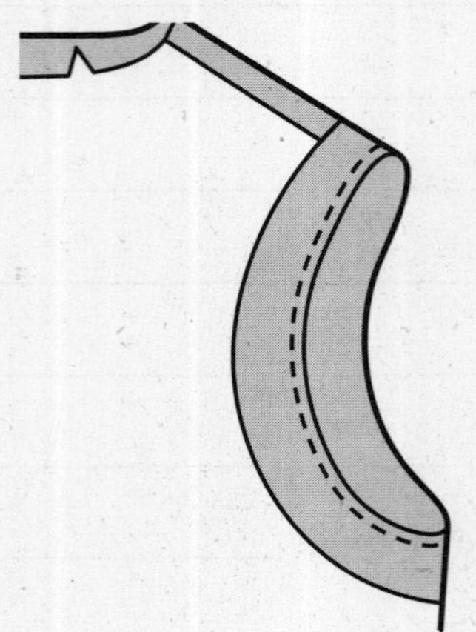

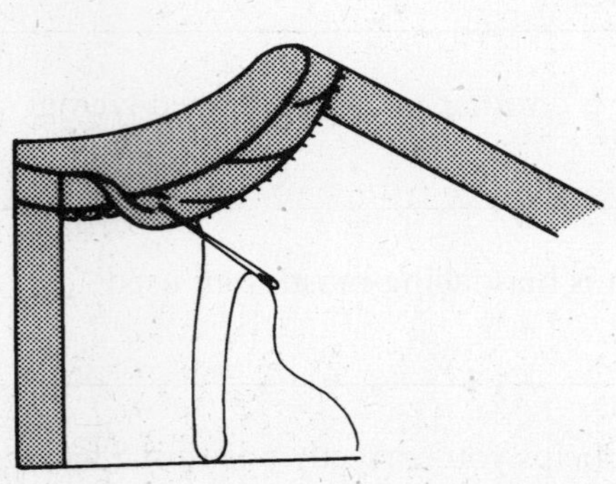

1. ____   2. ____

______   3. A facing should not be visible from the outside of a shirt.

______   4. A shaped facing is slightly smaller than the area it is designed to cover.

______   5. Another name for a bias facing is a fitted facing.

______   6. Extended facings are often used along a front or back opening.

______   7. Finishing the outside edge of a facing is not recommended.

______   8. Facings may be understitched or topstitched.

______   9. Trimming, grading, notching, or clipping is unnecessary when a serger is used to attach the facing.

______   10. Instead of tacking a facing to a seam allowance with thread, liquid seam sealant may be used.

______   11. You need a separate pattern piece for an extended facing.

______   12. Understitching helps keep a facing from rolling to the garment's outside.

______   13. Bias facings work well on very bulky or sheer fabrics.

______   14. A bias facing is made from a pattern piece.

______   15. The notched edge of a facing piece should be stay-stitched.

Clothing: Fashion, Fabrics & Construction Student Activity Manual

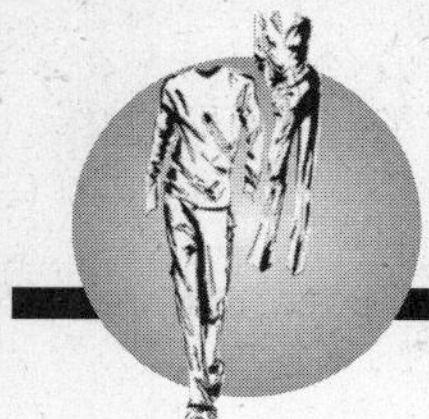

Making Casings

Directions: As you read the lesson, answer the following questions. Later you can use this study guide to review for the Part 4 Handbook test.

1. How can a casing be an alternative to a waistband? _______________________________

____

____

2. What are the two basic types of casings? _______________________________________

3. How long and wide should a fabric strip used for an applied casing be? ______________

____

____

4. How should the width of the elastic compare to the finished casing width? Why? ________

____

____

____

____

5. How can you figure the length of elastic needed for a casing if it is not given on the guide sheet? ________

____

____

____

6. How is an opening for drawstrings made? _______________________________________

____

____

____

7. How can you keep a drawstring from pulling out of a casing? _______________________

____

Casing Practice

Directions: Practice making a self-casing by constructing a simple, reusable gift bag. Choose a colorful scrap of fabric and follow the directions below. By varying the dimensions, you can make any size gift bag you choose.

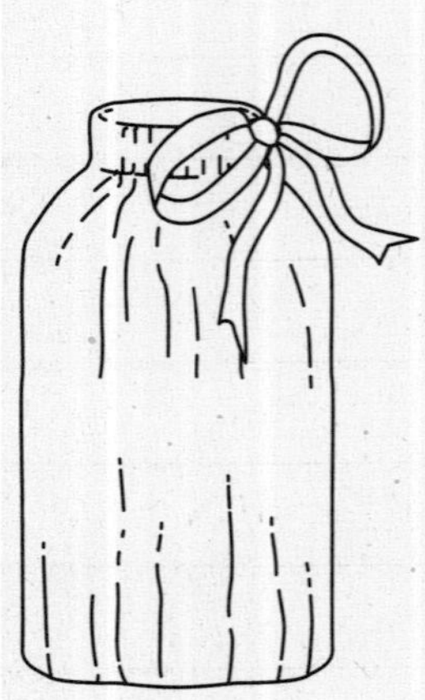

Drawstring Gift Bag

Equipment and Materials

- Woven fabric, approximately 14 × 14 inches (35.5 × 35.5 cm)
- Ribbon or yarn, 18 inches (46 cm)
- Shears
- Thread
- Tailor's chalk or fabric-marking pen
- Straight pins
- Safety pin
- Sewing gauge
- Ruler
- Sewing machine
- Serger (optional)
- Iron

Procedure

1. Fold the fabric in half. Mark a rectangle 6 × 12 inches (15 × 30.5 cm), with the fold as one side.
2. Cut out the rectangle. When opened, the fabric is a 12-inch (30.5-cm) square.
3. Mark a line 1¼ inches (3.2 cm) below the top edge. This will be the fold line for the casing at the top of the bag.
4. Fold the fabric in half, with **right** sides together and the casing line at the top. Pin the side and bottom seams. Serge or machine-stitch these two seams, using a ½-inch (1.3-cm) seam allowance. **Do not sew over pins.**
5. Turn the upper edge down, **wrong** sides together, along the fold line to form the casing. Press.
6. Turn the raw edge of the casing under ¼ inch (6 mm). Pin in place to the bag.
7. Starting at the side seam, machine-stitch close to the ¼-inch (6-mm) folded edge. To leave an opening in the casing, stop stitching about 1 inch before returning to the side seam. Backstitch to reinforce. Turn the bag right side out.
8. Attach a safety pin to the ribbon or yarn and feed through the casing.
9. Press the bag, and tie the ends of the ribbon together.

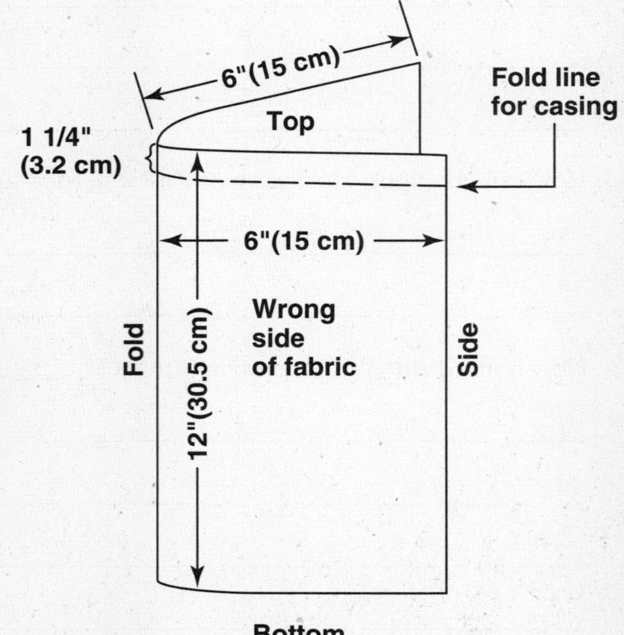

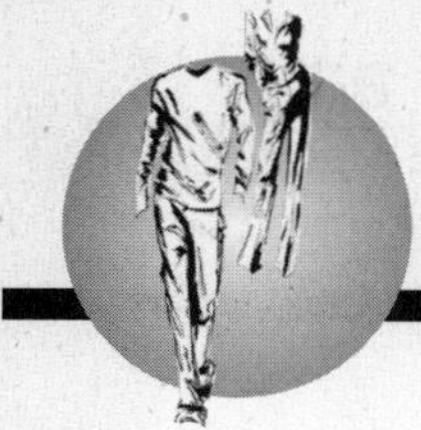

Applying Fasteners

Directions: As you read the lesson, answer the following questions. Later you can use this study guide to review for the Part 4 Handbook test.

1. Give two tips for hand-sewing fasteners.____

____

2. Why are hooks and eyes sewn only to the facing fabric?____________________________

____

3. Describe one way to mark the position of the socket half of a snap. _________________

____

____

____

4. Name three types of buttonholes. Which type is most common? _____________________

____

____

5. What three measurements determine buttonhole length? ___________________________

____

6. Describe the three lines used to mark buttonholes. _______________________________

____

____

7. Explain how to mark button locations. ____

____

____

8. Why might you use a toothpick to attach sew-through buttons? _____________________

____

____

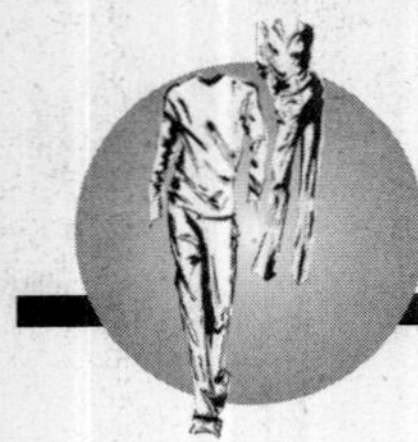

Buttonhole Math

Lesson 20
Activity

Directions: Each of the buttons below needs to have a buttonhole made for it. Your job is to determine the length each buttonhole should be. The length of a buttonhole is determined by the diameter and the thickness of the button. Using the information given, determine the buttonhole length for each button. Calculate the length for two different thicknesses, as shown in the chart.* Then write your answers in the last two columns.

Button Diameter + Button Thickness = Buttonhole Length

Button Sizes	Buttonhole Length for Thickness A: ⅛" (.3 cm)	Buttonhole Length for Thickness B: ¼" (.6 cm)
1 — ⅜" (1 cm)	⅜" (1 cm) + A =	⅜" (1 cm) + B =
2 — ½" (1.3 cm)	½" (1.3 cm) + A =	½" (1.3 cm) + B =
3 — ⅝" (1.5 cm)	⅝" (1.5 cm) + A =	⅝" (1.5 cm) + B =
4 — ¾" (2 cm)	¾" (2 cm) + A =	¾" (2 cm) + B =
5 — ⅞" (2.2 cm)	⅞" (2.2 cm) + A =	⅞" (2.2 cm) + B =
6 — 1" (2.5 cm)	1" (2.5 cm) + A =	1" (2.5 cm) + B =

* Centimeter measurements may vary slightly due to rounding.

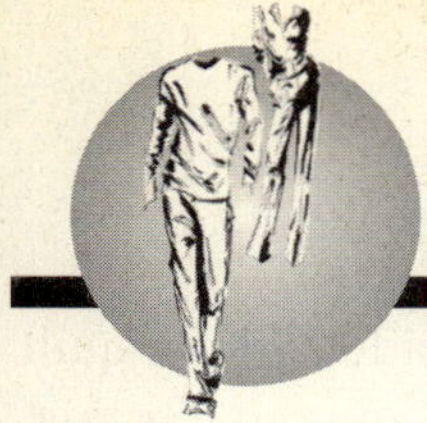

Fastener Practice

Directions: Use colorful scraps of leftover, washable fabrics to create this activity "snake" for a young child three years of age or older. Playing with fasteners on this colorful snake will help a child develop fine motor coordination. Use the directions that follow to create your snake. Make sure that the fasteners are applied securely so the child will not be able to remove them. Follow the sewing guidelines in Lesson 20 of your text for attaching all fasteners. (See **Fig. 20-a.**)

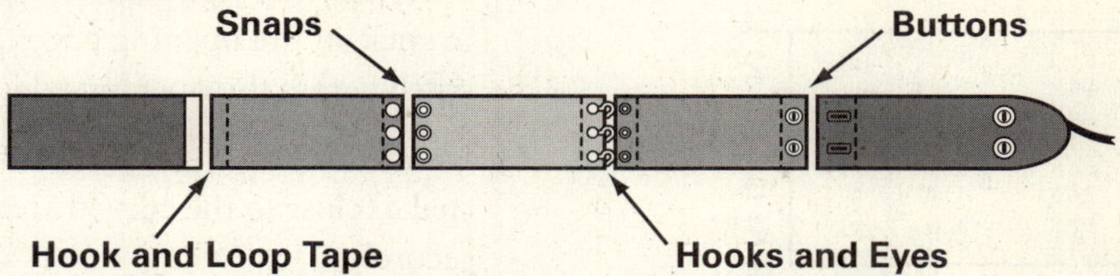

Materials and Equipment
- Eight rectangles of fabric (from scraps), 7 inches × 10 inches (18 cm × 25.5 cm)
- Two rectangles of fabric, 7 inches × 14 inches (18 cm × 35.5 -cm)
- Four rectangles of lightweight quilt batting, 7 inches × 10 inches (18 cm × 25.5 cm)
- One rectangle of lightweight quilt batting, 7 inches × 14 inches (18 cm × 35.5 cm)
- One strip of red felt for tongue, ½ inch × 3 inches (1 cm × 7.5 cm)
- Two large shank buttons for eyes (at least 1 inch or 2.5 cm)

- Three flat buttons, 1 inch (2.5 cm)
- Four large snaps (at least size 4)
- Four large hooks and eyes (at least size 3)
- One strip of hook-and-loop tape, 4 inches (10 cm) long
- Thread for machine
- Double-sided basting tape
- Tailor's chalk
- Sewing gauge
- Sewing machine

Procedure

Use ½-inch (1.3-cm) seam allowances throughout. Backstitch at the beginning and ending of all seams.

1. Cut eight rectangles of fabric, 7 inches × 10 inches (18 cm × 25.5 cm). Cut four rectangles of lightweight quilt batting the same size.

2. Cut two rectangles of fabric, 7 inches × 14 inches (18 cm × 35.5 cm). Cut one rectangle of lightweight quilt batting the same size. Round off one end of all layers of this rectangle to form the head of the snake. (see **Fig. 20-b.**)

3. With right sides together, layer the eight 7-inch × 10-inch (18-cm × 25.5-cm) rectangles together to form four pairs. Put one piece of quilt batting on

top of each rectangle pair and pin together, evenly matching all edges. These rectangles will form the body of the activity snake.

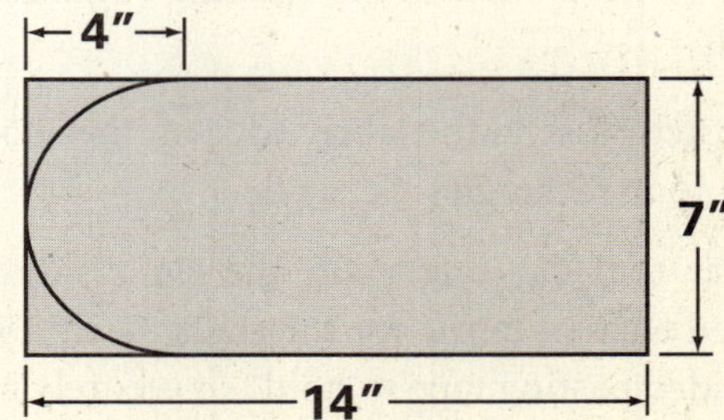

(continued on next page)

Chapter 20
Activity (continued)

4. Turn these 7-inch × 10-inch (18-cm × 25.5-cm) rectangle pairs over so that the fabric side faces up. On one 7-inch (18-cm) edge of each rectangle pair, use the tailor's chalk to mark a 3-inch (7.5-cm) opening to allow for turning the rectangles right-side out after stitching. Put the chalk markings 2 inches (5 cm) from each edge as indicated below. (See **Fig. 20-c.**)

5. Machine-stitch the snake body rectangles together. Begin at one of the markings, stitch around each rectangle—pivoting at each corner—and ending at the second marking (for opening).
   [*Note:* To pivot at the corners, stop the machine with the needle in the corner of the fabric, lift the presser foot and turn the fabric 90 degrees and line up on the ½-inch (1.3-cm) stitching guide on the machine. Continue stitching to the next corner and repeat.] (See **Fig. 20-d.**)

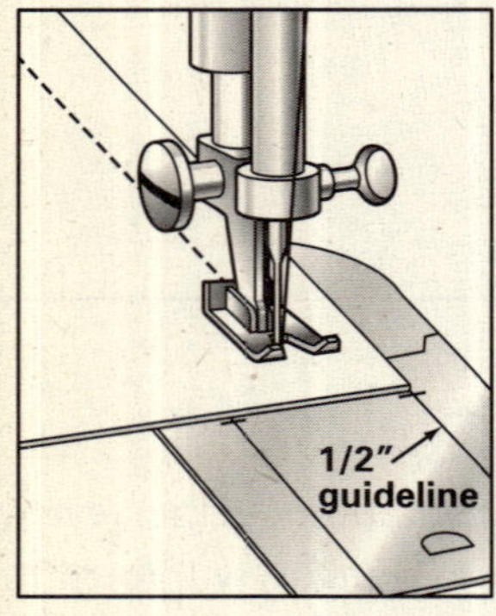

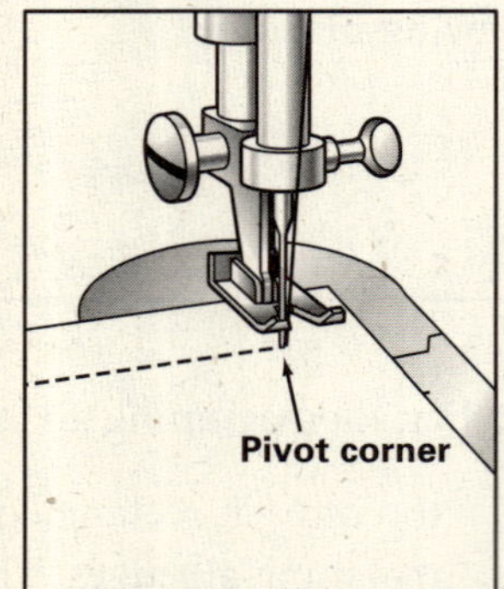

6. Turn the four rectangles right-side-out and press flat. Be sure to tuck-in the opening edges and press evenly.

7. Topstitch close to the fabric edge on the short sides of all four rectangles. Set aside.

8. Center the felt tongue on the right side of one curved edge of fabric for the snake head. Use double-sided basting tape to hold felt securely in place. Place the second layer of fabric for the head right side down on top of the tongue side. Put the quilt batting on top of the fabric layers and pin together, evenly matching all edges.

9. Machine-stitch the head together along all sides, beginning at one side of the opening and ending at the other side of the opening.

10. Turn the head right-side-out and press flat. Be sure to tuck-in the opening edges and press. Then topstitch across the opening edge to close.

11. Hand-sew the shank buttons to the head of the snake (close to the curved area) for the eyes. Attach securely.

12. Mark three buttonholes to fit your buttons on the short side of the snake head opposite the tongue and eyes. Evenly space the buttonhole markings. Stitch the buttonholes following the directions in the instruction manual for your machine.

13. Align the snake head with one body rectangle and mark the button placement to match the buttonholes on the head. Hand-sew the buttons to the rectangle, using a thread shank on each button.

14. Align the first body rectangle with the second. Mark the placement for four hooks and eyes on each side and evenly space. Hand-sew the hooks to the first rectangle and hand-sew the eyes to the second rectangle.

15. Align the third body rectangle with the second. Mark the placement for four snaps on each short edge and evenly space. Separate the snaps. Hand-sew the all of the "sockets" to one fabric rectangle and hand-sew all of the "ball" snap parts to the other rectangle.

16. Align the last body rectangle with the third. Pin the "hook" side of the hook-and-loop tape to the short edge of the third rectangle. Pin the "loop" side of tape to a short edge of the last body rectangle. Machine-stitch around all edges of the hook-and-loop tape to secure it to the fabric.

17. Align all pieces of the activity snake with the correlating fastener parts. Secure all fasteners. Use as a gift for a young child.

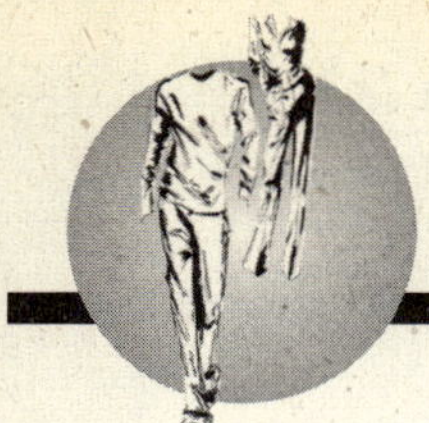

Putting in Zippers

Directions: As you read the lesson, answer the following questions. Later you can use this study guide to review for the Part 4 Handbook test.

1. How can you learn whether a particular zipper will work with a garment? ________________________________

____

2. Describe at least three steps that help prepare a fabric for applying a zipper. ________________________

____

____

____

____

3. In what two ways can zippers be applied? ____

____

____

4. Where can you choose the right application method? ____

____

5. How is a zipper positioned for a centered application? ____

____

____

6. When using the lapped application, how is the first side of the zipper positioned? __________________

____

____

7. How did the invisible zipper get its name? ____

____

____

8. How is an invisible zipper applied? ____

____

Zipper Application

Directions: Practice a centered zipper application by constructing this useful travel bag. Follow the directions below and refer to Lesson 21 in your textbook.

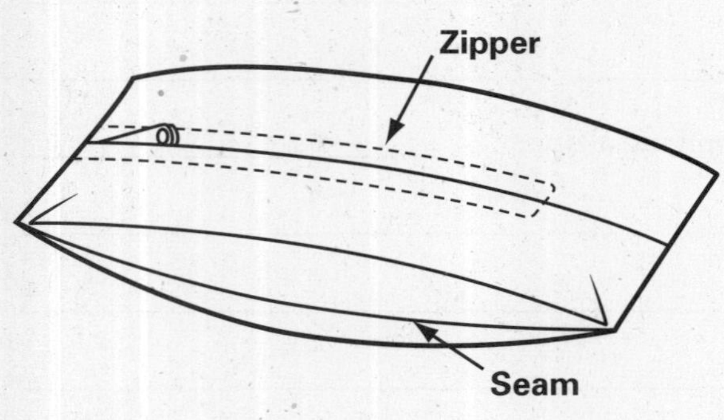

Travel Bag

Equipment and Materials

- Woven fabric, 10 × 20-inch (25.5 × 51-cm) scrap
- 7-inch (18-cm) zipper
- Shears
- Pins
- Tailor's chalk or fabric-marking pen
- Thread to match fabric
- Ruler
- Sewing machine with zipper foot
- Iron

Procedure

1. Measure and cut two pieces of fabric 10 × 5 inches (25.5 × 12.5 cm) and one piece 10 × 8 inches (25.5 × 20.5 cm).

2. Mark a dot 3 inches (7.5 cm) from one end on each of the two narrow pieces. This marks where the bottom of the zipper goes.

3. Place the two narrow pieces **right** sides together, matching the dot. Pin the long side with the dot.

4. Using a 1-inch (2.5-cm) seam allowance, stitch with a standard stitch from the bottom edge to the dot. Backstitch at the dot. Then machine-baste the rest of the seam to temporarily hold the zipper location closed.

5. Press the seam open. Then follow the instructions on pages 535-536 of your textbook to insert the zipper with a centered zipper application.

6. Open the zipper. Place the top of the travel bag (the section with the zipper) **right** sides together with the larger back piece, matching raw edges. Pin in place.

7. Machine-stitch, using a ⅝-inch (1.5-cm) seam allowance around all four sides of the bag. If desired, seam edges can be serged or trimmed with pinking shears to finish.

8. Trim the corners diagonally. Turn right side out through the zipper. Press.

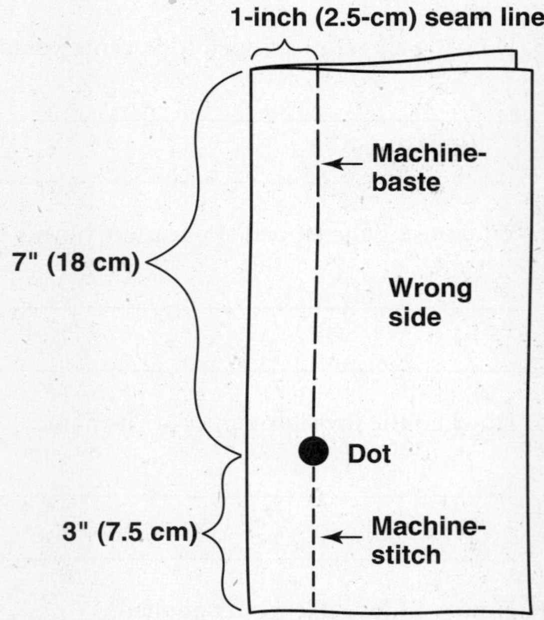

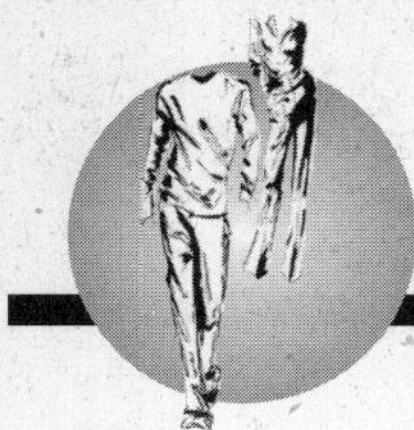

Putting in Hems

Directions: As you read the lesson, answer the following questions. Later you can use this study guide to review for the Part 4 Handbook test.

1. Give three tips for marking hems accurately. _______________________________________

   ____

   ____

   ____

2. How can you determine the right length for pants when marking hems? ______________________

   ____

3. What factors influence the recommended hem width on a pattern? _________________________

   ____

4. List four ways to finish the raw edge of a hem. ____

   ____

   ____

5. What are the advantages of blindstitching a hem? _______________________________________

   ____

6. How is fusible web positioned in a hem? Why? ____

   ____

   ____

   ____

7. How is a serger adjusted to make a rolled hem? ____

   ____

8. When might you decide to face a hem? ____

   ____

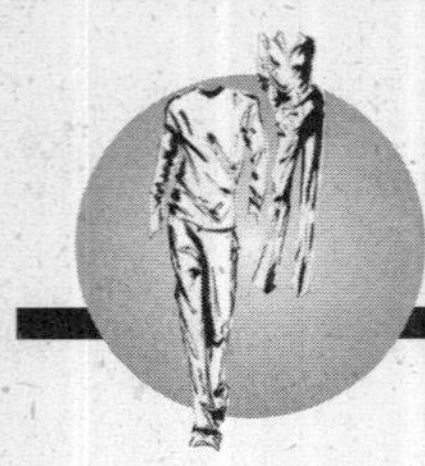

Hem Finishes

Directions: Identify the hem finishes and stitches shown below. Then cut four 3 × 3-inch (7.5 × 7.5-cm) squares of fabric. Fold up one edge of each, forming a 1-inch (2.5-cm) hem. Press. Apply seam tape to one of the samples. Refer to pages 506–510 and 538–540 to duplicate the hems depicted in the boxes below. Mount your finished samples on a separate sheet of paper and attach them to this worksheet.

1	2
3	4

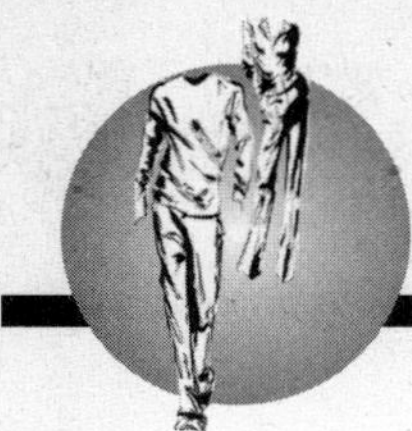

Checking the Fit

Directions: As you read the lesson, answer the following questions. Later you can use this study guide to review for the Part 4 Handbook test.

1. What are some signs that a handmade garment doesn't meet quality standards? _______________

____

____

____

2. When should you first try on a garment you are making? _______________

____

3. What should you do after making a change to improve a garment's fit? _______________

____

____

4. Describe a well-made neckline and collar. _______________

____

____

5. How should darts be positioned? _______________

____

6. Where should a waistline seam rest? _______________

____

____

7. What appearance and comfort points should you note in pants? _______________

____

____

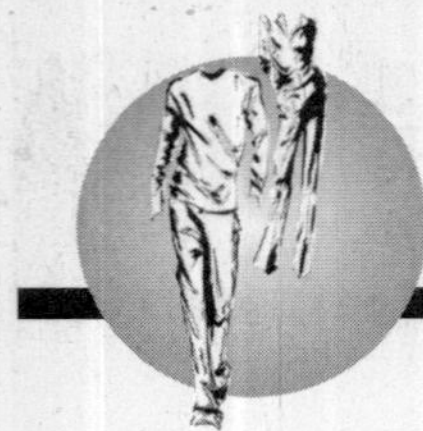

Evaluating Quality and Fit

Directions: Practice your ability to recognize quality and good fit. Examine a garment you own or a new one at a store. Try on the garment. Put a check mark next to each characteristic below that is true of the garment. Write "NA" if your garment doesn't have the specific feature, such as pockets or buttonholes.

_______ 1. Amount of fabric used does not seem skimpy.

_______ 2. The parts of the garment are cut and sewn so the garment hangs and moves well.

_______ 3. Collar and pockets lie flat.

_______ 4. Collar rolls evenly and collar points are identical.

_______ 5. Garment does not pull or wrinkle uncomfortably across the front or back.

_______ 6. Crotch length is comfortable for sitting.

_______ 7. Closings (zippers and rows of buttons) don't pull or gap.

_______ 8. Hem hangs evenly.

_______ 9. Buttons and other trim enhance the garment rather than detract from it.

_______ 10. Buttonholes are spaced evenly and completely finished.

_______ 11. Weave and finish of the fabric are unflawed.

_______ 12. Patterns and textures match at the seams.

_______ 13. There are no loose threads.

_______ 14. Thread color matches exactly or coordinates attractively.

_______ 15. There are no breaks, pulls, or gaps in the seams.

_______ 16. Seam allowances are generous.

_______ 17. Inside edges of the seams are finished carefully.

_______ 18. Hemline stitching is invisible.

_______ 19. It is comfortable to stand, sit, stretch, and bend in garment.

Conclusions

1. I rate the *quality* of this garment as:	2. I rate the *fit* of this garment as:	3. Given the price of this garment, I judge it to be:
_______ excellent	_______ excellent	_______ an excellent buy
_______ good	_______ good	_______ good quality for the money
_______ fair	_______ fair	_______ somewhat overpriced
_______ poor	_______ poor	_______ much too expensive

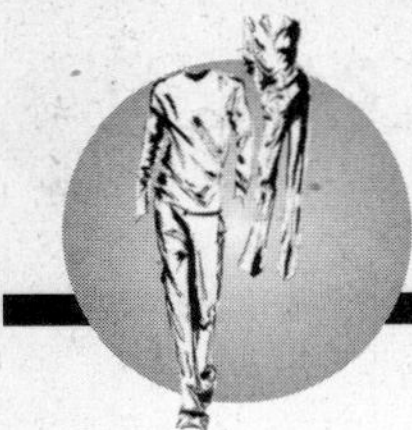

Sewing Special Seams

Directions: As you read the lesson, answer the following questions. Later you can use this study guide to review for the Part 5 Handbook test.

1. How does a French seam hide the raw seam edges? ___________________________________

____

____

2. How are seam allowances trimmed and stitched to make a flat-felled seam? ______________

____

____

3. How can you combine a conventional seam with a serged seam to reinforce areas of stress? ______

____

____

4. What is the difference between the two methods of topstitching a seam? _________________

____

____

____

5. How is a lapped seam formed? When is it used? ___________________________________

____

____

____

6. What is the main difference between a piped seam and other seams? ____________________

____

7. How is a serger adjusted to make a mock flatlock seam? ____________________________

____

____

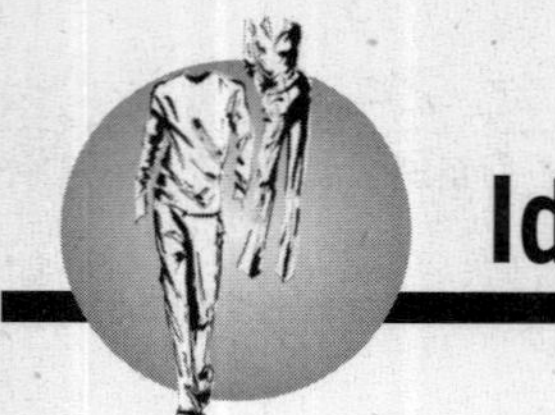

Identifying Special Seams

Directions: Ten special seams are listed below. Read the descriptions of special seams that follow. Write the name of the seam that matches the description. Note that some seams will be used more than once. Then choose and create samplers of at least four special seams. Use two, 3- × 6-inch (7.5-× 15-cm) pieces of fabric for each sampler. Mount your samplers on separate paper and label each with the name of the seam. Attach your samplers to this activity sheet.

Special Seams		
Double-stitched seam	Lapped seam	Reinforced seam
Flat-felled seam	Narrow rolled seam	Topstitched seam
Flatlock seam	Piped or corded seam	Welt seam
French seam		

______________________ 1. This seam provides a tailored finish on heavier fabrics.

______________________ 2. This seam is often used for armhole and crotch seams.

______________________ 3. This seam is created with a serger on sheer and lightweight fabrics.

______________________ 4. No raw edges show through the fabric because the tuck is on the wrong side of this seam.

______________________ 5. This seam is used when one piece is lapped over the other and top-stitched in place.

______________________ 6. This seam has a ladder-like appearance on one side of the garment and loops on the other.

______________________ 7. Used to emphasize seams in a garment, this seam also holds bulky seam allowances flat.

______________________ 8. This seam is often used on natural or synthetic leather and suede.

______________________ 9. This heavy-duty seam involves using the sewing machine and serger.

______________________ 10. This sturdy seam is likely to be found on denim jeans.

______________________ 11. Stitching can be done on one or both sides of this seam.

______________________ 12. A zipper foot is used to create this decorative seam.

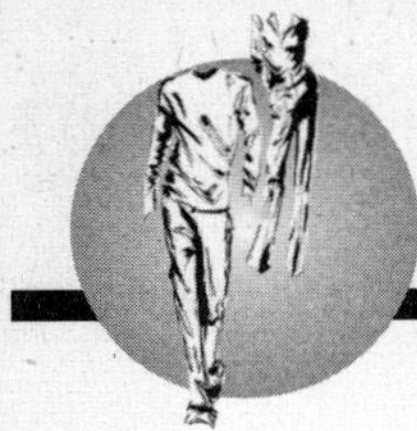

Making Tucks and Pleats

Directions: As you read the lesson, answer the following questions. Later you can use this study guide to review for the Part 5 Handbook test.

1. What functional and decorative purposes do tucks and pleats serve? _______________________________

____

____

2. How does a pattern distinguish between pin tucks and wide tucks? _______________________________

____

____

3. How can you quickly distinguish fold lines from stitching lines when marking tucks? ______________

____

____

4. How can you achieve decorative effects when stitching tucks on a serger?______________________

____

____

5. How can you avoid leaving impressions on the outside of a garment when pressing pleats? _________

____

____

6. What should you do to press pleats into soft folds? Into sharp creases?_____________________

____

____

7. How do topstitching and edgestitching affect pleats? _________________________________

____

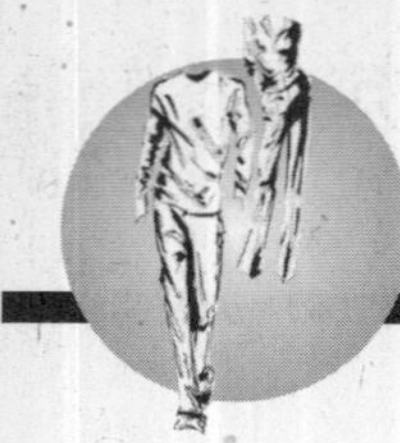

Identifying Tucks and Pleats

Directions: Fill in the blanks to complete the statements about the tucks and pleats shown below.

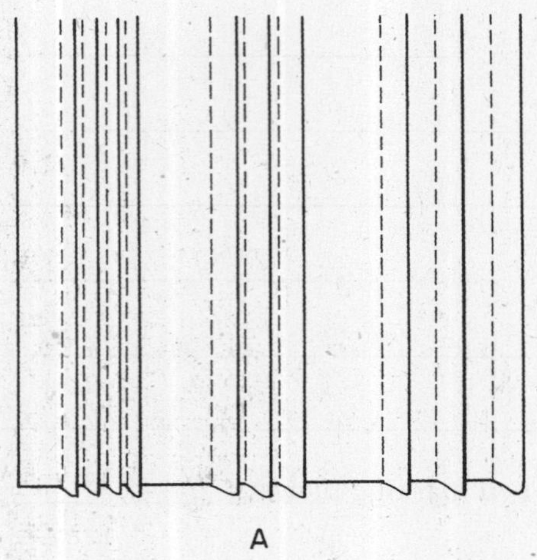

A

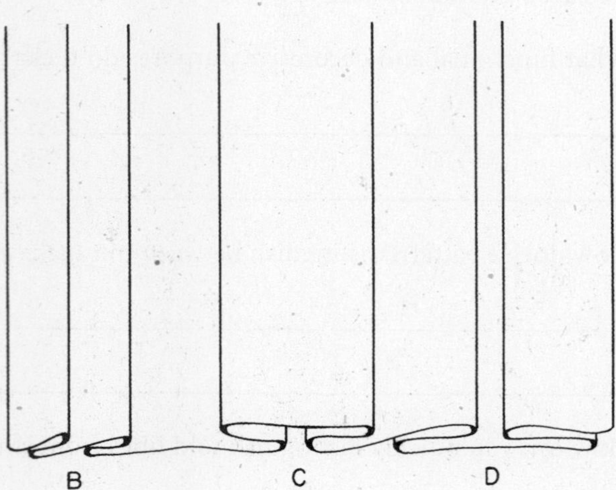

B   C   D

1. Figure A shows _______________________.

2. Figure B shows _______________________.

3. Figure C shows _______________________.

4. Figure D shows _______________________.

5. Instead of marking lines on fabric to make tucks, you can save time by marking with

_______________________ and _______________________.

6. To add tucks to a pattern, you need to purchase _______________________ fabric.

7. Pleats that are turned toward each other are called _______________________ and

_______________________.

8. It is possible to use the serger for making _______________________, but not _______________________.

9. When pressing pleats, use a(n) _______________________.

10. Before edgestitching the pleats of a skirt, complete the _______________________ of the garment.

11. When a pleat is _______________________, it is usually done only between the waist and hip area.

12. Stitch each _______________________ from the side that will be seen.

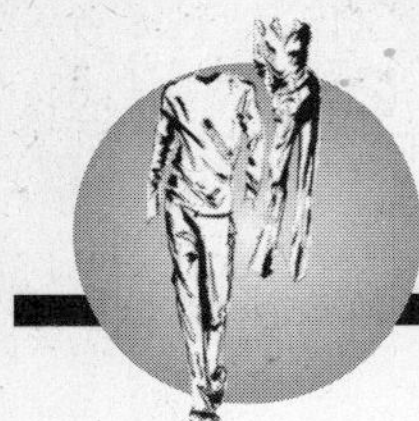

Applying Interfacings

Directions: As you read the lesson, answer the following questions. Later you can use this study guide to review for the Part 5 Handbook test.

1. Where would you use interfacing on a dress shirt? Why? _______________________________________

____

____

____

2. What do you use as a guide to cut interfacing for a waistband if no piece is included in the pattern?

____

3. What are the two main types of interfacing? ____

4. In what ways should interfacing match the garment fabric? ____________________________________

____

____

5. How is sew-in facing sewn to a garment? ____

____

____

____

6. What two things can you learn by pretesting fusible interfacing? _______________________________

____

____

7. Briefly explain how to apply fusible interfacing.____

____

____

____

____

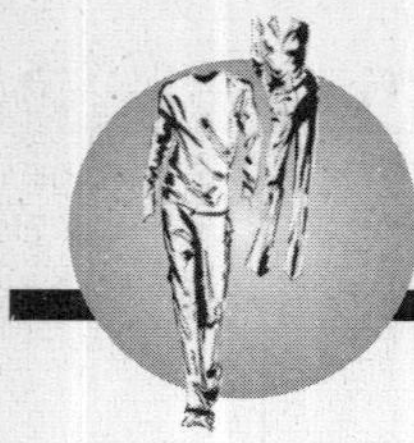

Comparing Interfacings

Lesson 26
Activity

Directions: Cut two small rectangles of fabric, each about 2 × 5 inches (5 × 12.5 cm). Following the first three steps of the directions on text page 553, apply sew-in interfacing to one fabric piece. Apply fusible interfacing to the other piece, as directed on page 554. Secure the samples to this worksheet and answer the questions below.

Sew-In Interfacing

Fusible Interfacing

Conclusions

1. Which application process did you find easier? Explain. ________________________________

____

____

____

2. If you were constructing a garment from this fabric, which interfacing would you use? Would you choose the same weight? Explain.

____

____

____

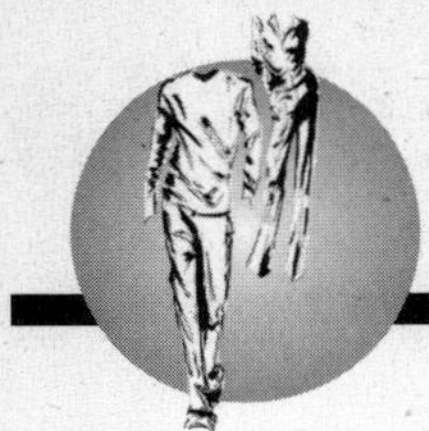

Putting in Linings

Directions: As you read the lesson, answer the following questions. Later you can use this study guide to review for the Part 5 Handbook test.

1. Why might a lining be added to a garment? _______________________________________

____

____

____

____

2. How can you decide whether a color is a good choice for a lining fabric? ______________

____

____

3. What types of garments are likely to have separate pattern pieces for lining? __________

____

4. Do you need to finish seams when stitching together lining pieces? __________________

____

5. How do a skirt lining and jacket lining differ in construction? ______________________

____

____

6. Explain how to attach a lining to a garment hem. _______________________________

____

____

____

____

____

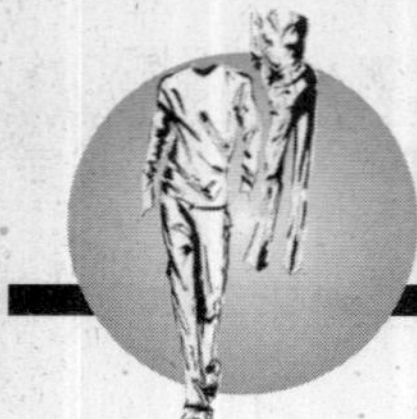

Questions About Linings

Directions: Imagine that you handle questions about clothing care and sewing for an Internet Web site. Read the following questions that have been submitted and respond to them on the lines provided.

1. I got drenched in a rainstorm while wearing my favorite coat. After having it cleaned, the lining now hangs longer than the coat itself! How can that be? What should I do?

____

____

____

2. I am sewing a costume for the girl who has the lead in our school musical. The pale peach fabric is really pretty, but it is fairly delicate. I am afraid you will be able to see through to the darker lining fabric that we have on hand. What would you do?

____

____

____

3. The blazer I have decided to sew is supposed to have a center-back pleat. It would be simpler and less time consuming not to have a pleat. What do you think?

____

____

____

4. My brother and I are both making lined vests. He is serging all the seams of the vest and the lining. I really do not see that it is a necessary step. Who is correct?

____

____

____

5. I am not sure what to look for when I shop for lining fabric for my sewing project. Do you have any tips? For instance, should the color be a perfect match?

____

____

____

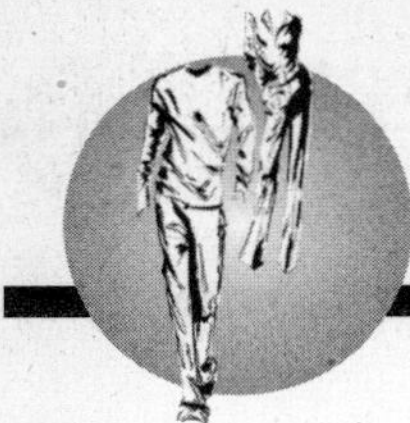

Sewing Collars

Directions: As you read the lesson, answer the following questions. Later you can use this study guide to review for the Part 5 Handbook test.

1. How is a rolled collar cut? ____

____

____

2. What separates a shirt collar from the garment neckline? ___________________

____

3. Describe the qualities of a well-made collar. ____________________________

____

____

____

4. How is interfacing attached during construction of a one-piece collar?_________

____

____

5. How can you make strong, crisp points on a collar? ________________________

____

____

6. When constructing a collar, how can you prevent the edges of the under collar from showing?

____

____

7. What kinds of collars are sewn without a facing? With a partial facing? __________

____

____

Identifying Collars

Directions: Complete the chart below by providing the missing information. If the illustration is missing, sketch the collar described.

Description	Illustration
1. Collar name: ________________________ _______________________ _______________________ _______________________ _______________________	
2. Collar name: _Flat collar_______________ _______________________ _______________________ _______________________ _______________________	
3. Collar name: ________________________ Has separate band that attaches collar to neckline. _______________________ _______________________	
4. Collar name: ________________________ _______________________ _______________________ _______________________	

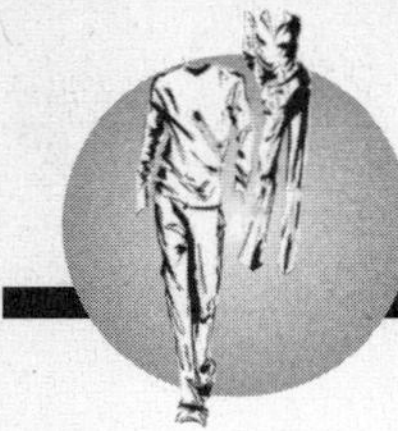

Sewing Sleeves

Lesson 29
Study Guide

Directions: As you read the lesson, answer the following questions. Later you can use this study guide to review for the Part 5 Handbook test.

1. How is a set-in sleeve different from a raglan sleeve? ___________________________________

____

____

2. Describe a kimono sleeve. ____

____

3. Why are set-in sleeves more difficult to sew than others? _______________________________

____

____

4. When can you use the open-sleeve method? ____

____

5. Why is the open-sleeve method also called the flat construction method? ___________________

____

6. Why is the closed-sleeve method also called the unit method? ____________________________

____

7. How is fullness in the cap sleeve adjusted in closed-sleeve construction? ___________________

____

____

____

8. What gives a raglan sleeve shape over the shoulder? ___________________________________

9. What serger stitches are useful for constructing and attaching sleeves? ____________________

____

____

____

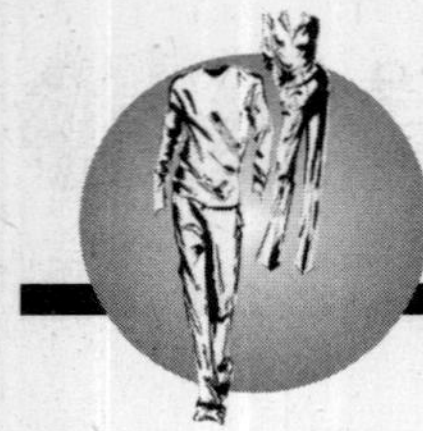

Identifying Sleeves

Directions: Identify the sleeves in the illustrations below. Then answer the questions that follow about the three basic sleeve styles.

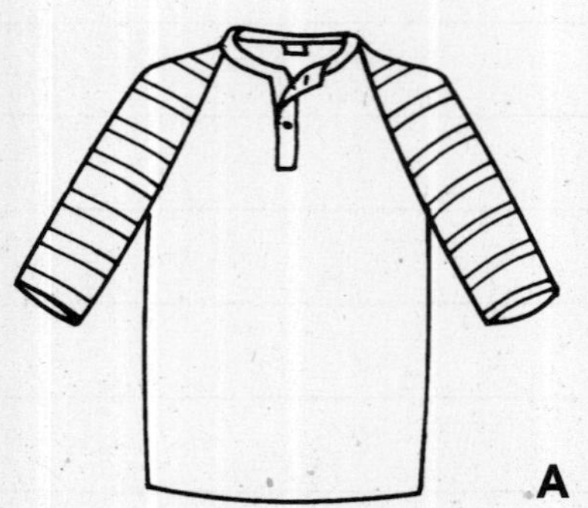

A

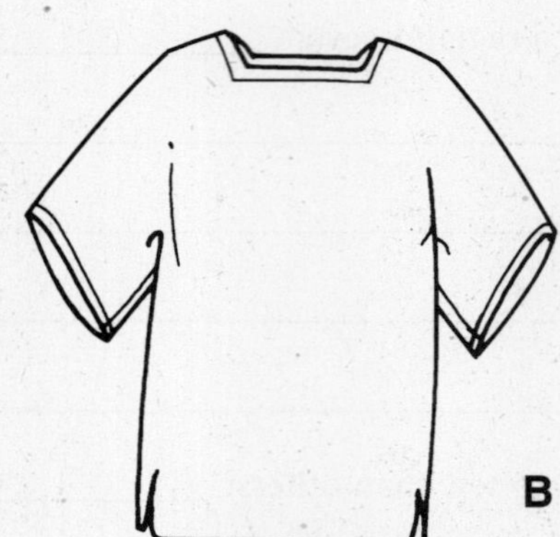

B

C

1. Figure A shows _________________________ sleeves.

2. Figure B shows _________________________ sleeves.

3. Figure C shows _________________________ sleeves.

4. The _________________________ sleeve is easy for beginning sewers to make because it is cut in one piece with the front and back of the garment.

5. When a set-in sleeve needs very little easing, you may use the sewing technique called the

    _________________________ method.

6. The only sleeve that contains a dart is the _________________________ sleeve.

7. Seam tape is used to reinforce the seam of the _________________________ sleeve.

8. To create puff sleeves on a toddler girl's dress, follow the steps of the _________________________

    method for _________________________ sleeves.

9. A soft flannel baby gown is usually constructed with _________________________ sleeves.

10. The sleeves on the garment you are wearing today are the _________________________ style.

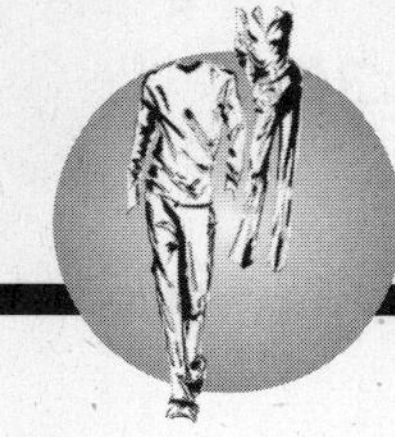

Sewing Cuffs

Directions: As you read the lesson, answer the following questions. Later you can use this study guide to review for the Part 5 Handbook test.

1. How is sewing a fold-up cuff similar to sewing a hem? How is it different? _______________________

____

____

____

2. What kind of cuff needs a placket? Why? ____

____

3. When during sleeve construction is a placket sewn? ____________________________________

____

4. What is used to finish the opening in a faced placket? In a continuous lap placket? ___________

____

____

5. How are the underlap and overlap added to a banded placket? ___________________________

____

____

____

6. How are cuff edges positioned for a shirtsleeve opening? For other openings? ________________

____

____

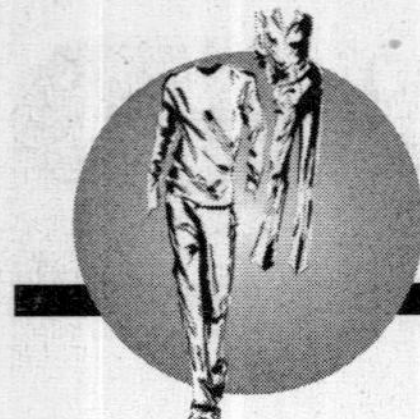

Cuff Construction

Directions: Select the answer that best completes each statement below. Write the letter of your answer in the blank provided at the left.

_______ 1. Patterns with cuffs are __?__.
A. not a good choice for beginning sewers
B. most likely to be found for children's garments
C. slowly being replaced by sleeves featuring elastic

_______ 2. When constructing a fold-up cuff, __?__.
A. plan ahead for buttonhole placement
B. slash the placket very carefully
C. tack the cuff to the seams

_______ 3. It is necessary for band cuffs to be __?__.
A. interfaced or sprayed with starch
B. large enough for the wearer's hand to pass through
C. finished with seam binding

_______ 4. A placket may be used for an opening __?__.
A. instead of a dart
B. when a casual look is desired
C. at a neckline, waist, or wrist

_______ 5. The three types of plackets used for sleeves are __?__.
A. banded, folded, and buttoned
B. banded, faced, and continuous lap
C. all relatively simple to construct

_______ 6. A buttoned cuff requires __?__.
A. fewer sewing notions than other cuffs
B. a buttonhole attachment for the sewing machine
C. a placket

_______ 7. Hook-and-loop tape could be substituted for __?__.
A. a button in a buttoned cuff
B. a fastener in a band cuff
C. the interfacing in a cuff

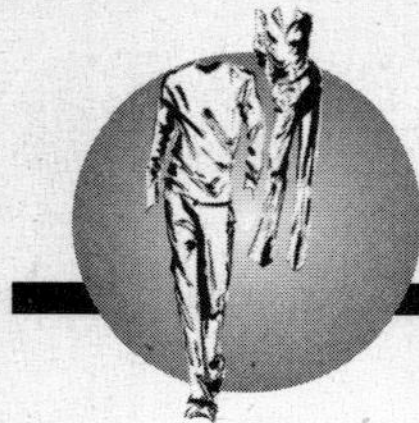

Sewing Pockets

Directions: As you read the lesson, answer the following questions. Later you can use this study guide to review for the Part 5 Handbook test.

1. How might you need to adjust a pattern when adding a pocket? _______________________________

____

____

2. What are three possible ways to cut an in-seam pocket? ___________________________________

____

____

3. Do patch pockets need a lining? Explain. ____

____

4. What kind of pockets are mitered? Why? ____

____

5. How are curved edges on pockets eased in? ____

____

____

____

6. How are thread tensions adjusted to serge a curved patch pocket? __________________________

____

____

____

7. What fabrics are used to cut the back section and front section of a front hip pocket? Why? ________

____

____

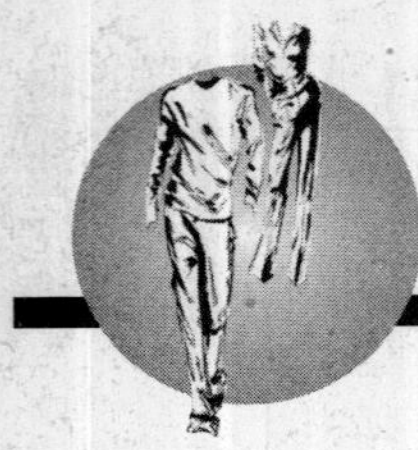

Pocket Identification

Directions: Read each statement below and identify the pocket it describes. Write the name of one of these pocket types in the space provided: *patch*, *in-seam*, or *front hip*.

______________________ 1. In evaluating a garment, you think these pockets look bulky and uneven. You suspect they have not been mitered.

______________________ 2. A sewing instructor recommends this type of pocket on the first garment projects for beginning students.

______________________ 3. Because she was using a sturdy gabardine, one teen decided to leave this pocket unlined.

______________________ 4. After finishing a garment's waistline, a teen realized it was too late to add these pockets.

______________________ 5. If your garment is made from denim or corduroy, you will need to cut these pocket pieces from a lining fabric.

______________________ 6. You sometimes need to notch the lower edges to give these pockets a smooth appearance.

______________________ 7. After cutting the fabric for this pocket, a teen discovered that the stripes on the pocket did not match those on the shirt.

______________________ 8. While laying out a pattern, you might find that this pocket is cut as part of the garment pieces.

______________________ 9. Some people like this pocket as is; others like a flap sewn above it.

______________________ 10. This pocket is sewn as a pouch entirely on the inside of the garment.

______________________ 11. The upper edge of these pockets illustrates using curved and diagonal lines in garment design.

______________________ 12. In a creative move, one designer used both curved and square versions of this pocket in the same garment.

______________________ 13. You can use lining fabric for the front section of these pockets, but not the back.

______________________ 14. Since it is hidden from sight, you can sew this pocket completely from lining fabric.

______________________ 15. Unlike the other types, this pocket is cut from one piece of fabric.

______________________ 16. This pocket is sometimes cut on the bias to add design interest.

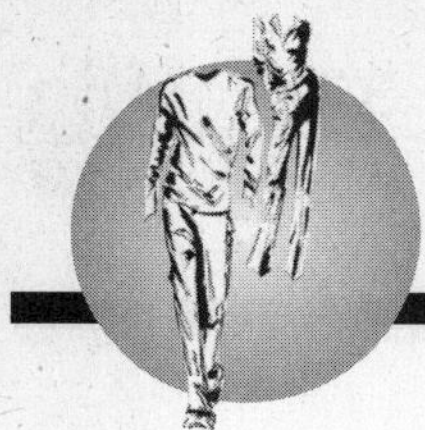

Finishing Waistlines

Directions: As you read the lesson, answer the following questions. Later you can use this study guide to review for the Part 5 Handbook test.

1. In what three ways can a garment waistline be finished? ________________________________

   ____

2. How are comfort and a smooth fit created in a waistband? ________________________________

   ____

   ____

3. If a front zipper overlaps right over left, how does the waistband overlap? How do you know this?

   ____

4. What is a stay? From what materials might a stay be made? ________________________________

   ____

   ____

5. When is serging a waistband especially useful? Why? ________________________________

   ____

   ____

6. How are the basic procedures for sewing and attaching a plain waistband and a topstitched waistband
   different?

   ____

   ____

   ____

   ____

7. How is the waistband matched correctly to the garment? ________________________________

   ____

8. Why is a facing added to a garment waistline? ________________________________

   ____

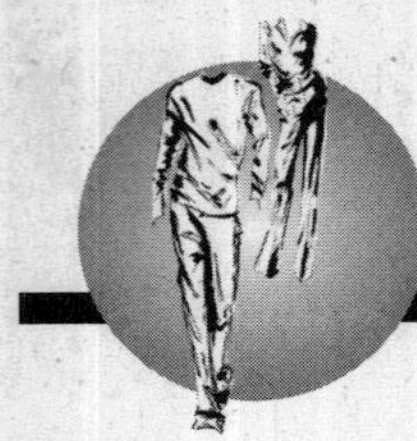

Waistband Checkup

Directions: Read each statement below. If the statement is correct, put a plus (+) in the space to the left. If it is incorrect, cross out the word or words in italics and write the word or words that make the statement true in the space provided.

__________________________ 1. A plain waistband is first attached to the garment's *right* side.

__________________________ 2. A plain waistband is first attached to the garment with *hand* stitching.

__________________________ 3. A *casing* is an alternative to a plain or topstitched waistband.

__________________________ 4. Most garment waistlines fall *above* the natural waistline.

__________________________ 5. When interfacing a waistband, the interfacing is usually attached to the side of the waistband that will be on the *inside* of the garment.

__________________________ 6. A waistband should measure about *1 inch (2.5 cm)* longer than the actual waistline.

__________________________ 7. A topstitched waistband is first attached to the garment's *wrong* side.

__________________________ 8. A *stay* is a piece of fabric tape or ribbon used to prevent stretching at the waistline.

__________________________ 9. A waistband is usually sewn to a garment *before* a zipper is attached.

__________________________ 10. Applying interfacing is the *last* step in making a waistband.

__________________________ 11. The overlap of a waistband that opens on the side faces the *back* of the garment.

__________________________ 12. A waistband is completed *before* it's sewn on a garment.

__________________________ 13. A stay is sewn onto the garment's *seam allowance*.

__________________________ 14. A waistband may be attached to a pair of shorts or pants, or to a *dress*.

__________________________ 15. Buttons or snaps are attached to a waistband *after* the waistband is completely sewn onto the garment.

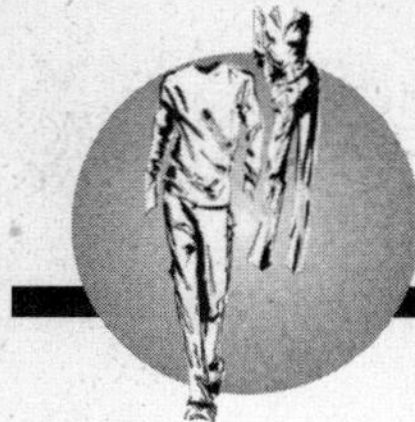

Applying Bias Bindings

Directions: As you read the lesson, answer the following questions. Later you can use this study guide to review for the Part 5 Handbook test.

1. List different uses for bias bindings. ____

   ____

   ____

   ____

2. Which method for cutting bias bindings is better to finish the edges of a three-foot-long wall hanging: continuous or cut-and-piece? Why?

   ____

3. What binding materials are applied using the one-step method? The two-step method? __________________

   ____

   ____

   ____

4. How can you pre-shape binding before stitching on curves? ____________________

   ____

   ____

5. How wide should you cut a bias strip of fabric for piping? ____________________

   ____

   ____

6. Why is a zipper foot used to make corded piping? ____________________________

   ____

7. How is a serger used to make tubing? ____

   ____

   ____

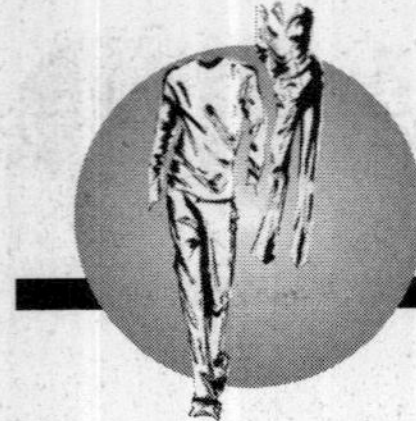

About Bias Bindings

Part I. Directions: Read each of the following statements about bias bindings. Place a plus (+) in the blank beside the true statements. Place a zero (0) in the space beside the false statements.

_______ 1. Bias bindings get their name because they are cut from fabric on the bias.

_______ 2. Bindings may be made from either woven or knitted fabric.

_______ 3. Extra fullness in curved bias strips shrinks out when the garment is washed.

_______ 4. If you cut your own bias strips, you should attach them using the two-step method.

_______ 5. You need strips at least 2 inches (5 cm) wide to make bias binding.

_______ 6. The continuous bias-strip method is recommended for cutting smaller lengths of bias strips.

_______ 7. A zipper foot is useful for making corded piping.

_______ 8. Piping is used to minimize a garment's seam lines.

_______ 9. Tubing is constructed inside out.

_______ 10. Bias bindings can be substituted for facing at the neckline or armhole of a garment.

_______ 11. To curve a bias binding, form a neat miter on both sides of the curve.

_______ 12. The cut-and-piece method is convenient for making longer bias strips.

_______ 13. Bias bindings can be used on garment corners.

_______ 14. Bindings are functional rather than decorative.

_______ 15. Fold-over braid trim can be used for binding.

_______ 16. A serger is most convenient for completing the two-step method.

_______ 17. Bias bindings may be used on belts and straps.

_______ 18. You should use the one-step method to attach double-fold tape.

_______ 19. To add thickness when trimming a seam, corded piping can be used.

_______ 20. The narrower tubing is, the easier it is to turn it right side out.

Part II. Directions: Create two binding samplers demonstrating the *one-step method* and the *two-step method* for attaching bias strips. Follow the directions for applying these bindings on page 575 of your textbook. Use 4- × 6-inch (10- × 15-cm) pieces of fabric for your samplers. Mount your samplers on separate sheets of paper. Attach your samplers to this activity sheet.

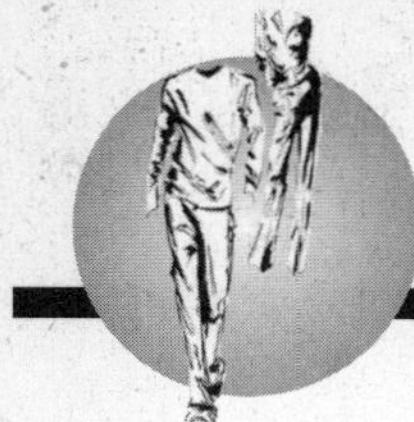

Adding Ruffles

Directions: As you read the lesson, answer the following questions. Later you can use this study guide to review for the Part 5 Handbook test.

1. From what are straight ruffles made? How are they made? _______________________________________

____

____

2. Why might you plan on using a longer piece of fabric to make wide ruffles than to make narrow ones?

____

____

3. How can you add fullness to lightweight or sheer ruffles? ______________________________________

____

____

4. How long should the fabric used for straight ruffles measure? __________________________________

____

____

5. How can you hide the gathering stitches on double-edge ruffles? ________________________________

____

6. How is a circular ruffle usually made? ____

____

7. Explain a technique for gathering ruffles when the gathers will be hidden in a seam. _______________

____

____

____

____

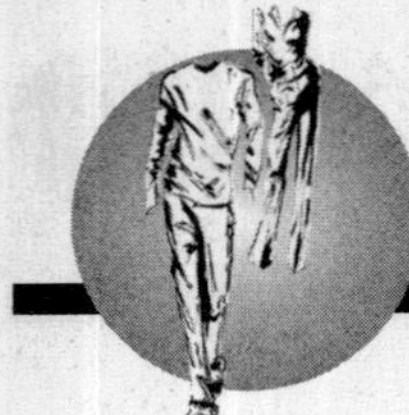

Making Ruffles

Directions: Look through pattern books or visit the Web site of a pattern company, paying special attention to projects that have ruffles. Find three patterns that feature at least one view with ruffles. Identify the type of project (window covering, home decorating item, garment, costume, etc.) and the type of ruffle. Place a check mark next to any pattern below if it's a project you would be interested in making. Then make two simple ruffles by following the directions under "Practice," and answer the questions.

1. Pattern maker and number ____

   Type of project ____

   Type of ruffle ____

2. Pattern maker and number ____

   Type of project ____

   Type of ruffle ____

3. Pattern maker and number ____

   Type of project ____

   Type of ruffle ____

Practice

Cut two strips of fabric, each 3 × 36 inches (7.5 × 91.5 cm). Follow Steps 1 and 2 of the directions on page 579 of the text. Adjust the gathers of one ruffle so the length of the piece is 18 inches (46 cm). Gather the second ruffle so its finished length is 12 inches (30.5 cm). Mount your samplers on separate sheets of paper and attach them to this activity.

1. How long did it take to construct the ruffles?____

   ____

2. Which ruffle do you prefer? Why? ____

   ____

   ____

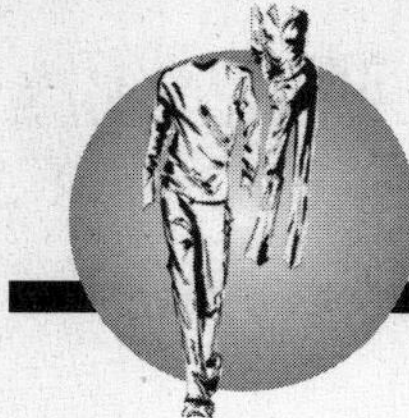

Adding Trims

Directions: As you read the lesson, answer the following questions. Later you can use this study guide to review for the Part 5 Handbook test.

1. Give two guidelines for choosing trim for a project. ____

____

____

2. How should you treat trim before using it? ____

____

____

3. Where can stitching be placed in the flat method of applying trim? ___________________________

____

4. What type of trim can be applied using the edging method? _________________________________

____

5. When is a serger useful for applying trim? ____

____

____

6. How is trim attached using the inserted method? ____

____

____

7. Describe three ways to finish the ends of trims. ____

____

____

____

____

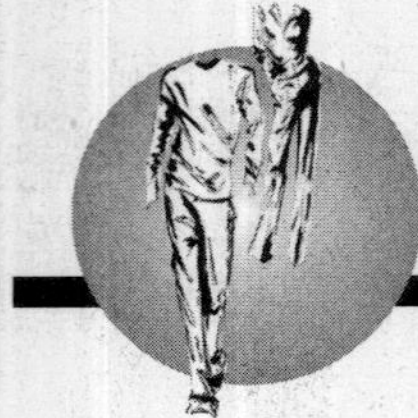

Comparing Trims

Part I. Directions: Visit a fabric store to observe trims, including fringe, piping, eyelet, lace, ribbon, braid, and rickrack. Make notes about six trims, filling in the information below. To calculate the cost per yard for packaged trims, divide the package price by the amount of trim contained in the package. Then answer the questions that follow.

1	**2**	**3**
Type __________	Type __________	Type __________
Cost per yard __________	Cost per yard __________	Cost per yard __________
Suitable for __________	Suitable for __________	Suitable for __________
4	**5**	**6**
Type __________	Type __________	Type __________
Cost per yard __________	Cost per yard __________	Cost per yard __________
Suitable for __________	Suitable for __________	Suitable for __________

1. Which trim listed above is the most expensive? The least expensive? ________________________________

____

2. Which trims would be applied using the flat method? ____

____

3. Which trims would be applied using the edging method? ______________________________________

____

4. Are there any trims that might be applied using the inserted method? Which ones? ________________

____

Part II. Directions: To extend this activity, select three of the trims listed above to practice your skills and create samplers. Follow the directions of applying trims on pages 581 to 583 of your textbook. Mount your samplers on separate sheets of paper and attach them to this activity.